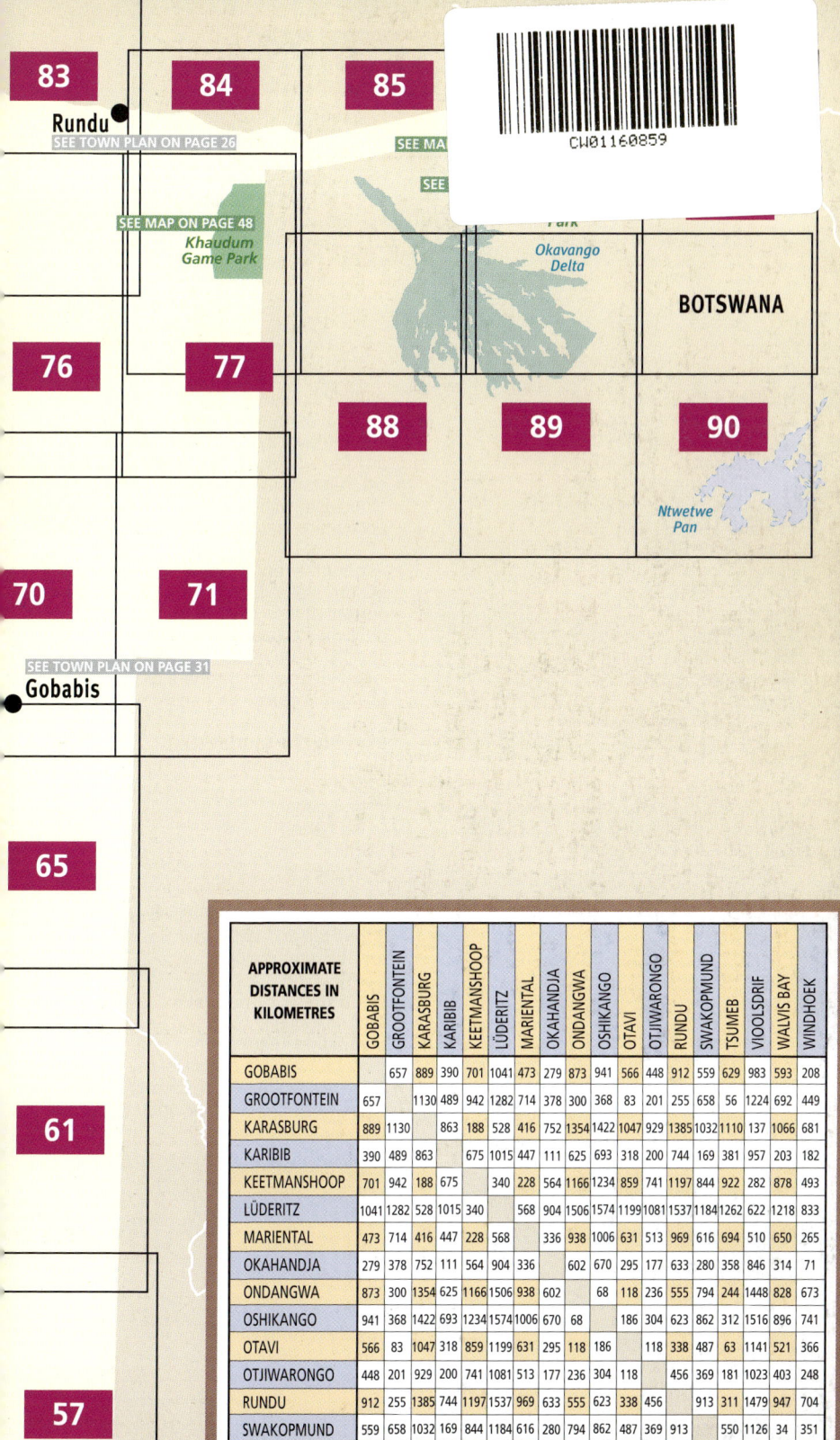

Third edition published in 2010 by Map Studio
www.mapstudio.co.za
0860 10 50 50

HEAD OFFICE
Cornelis Struik House
80 McKenzie Street
Cape Town
Tel: 021 462 4360

PO Box 1144
Cape Town, 8000

SALES OFFICES
Maps and Travel
Shop ST3A
Rivonia Village
Rivonia Boulevard
Rivonia
Tel: 011 807 5470
Fax: 011 807 7491

Map Studio Cape Town
Unit 7, M5 Freeway Park
Maitland (off Black River Parkway)
Tel: 021 510 4311
Fax: 021 510 4766

ISBN: 978-1-77026-169-3

Printed by CTP Cape Printers (Ltd)
ISO 12647 compliant

Copyright © 2010 in text: Map Studio™
Copyright © 2010 in maps: Map Studio™
Copyright © 2010 in photographs:
Photographers as credited (below)
Copyright © 2010 Map Studio™

Photographic Credits:
Jéan du Plessis: All images with the exception of:
Martin Harvey: p6 (top), 26, 42 (top)
Ian Michler: p8 (bottom)
Images of Africa /
  Nigel J. Dennis: p46
Images of Africa /
  Peter Pickford: p10 (bottom)
Willie & Sandra Olivier: p28

All rights reserved. No part of this publication may be reproduced, stored in a retrieval system or transmitted, in any form or by any means, electronic, mechanical, photocopying, recording or otherwise, without the permission of the publishers and copyright holders.

Although every effort has been made to ensure that this guide is up to date and current at time of going to print, the publisher accepts no responsibility or liability for any loss, injury or inconvenience incurred by readers or travellers using this guide.

Map Studio Tourist team:
Dénielle Lategan
Elaine Fick
John Loubser
Lois O'Brien
Myrna Collins
Ryan Africa

Special thanks to Claudia dos Santos, John Hall and Willie and Sandra Olivier for their contributions.

Been there, done that?
Please let us know if you find any interesting information on your travels through Namibia or notice any changes. We'll reward the 10 best contributions with a copy of this guide when we update it.

Send your contributions to:
research@mapstudio.co.za

NAMIBIA

Contents Contents Contents Conte

INTRODUCTION	**4**	**TOURIST AREAS**	**34**
History	6	Etosha	36
People	8	Sossusvlei / Namib-Naukluft Park	
Nature	10	(mountain region)	38
Activities	12	Kaokoland	40
		Fish River Canyon	42
TOWNS	**14**	Namib-Naukluft Park (desert)	
Windhoek	16	& West Coast	44
Daan Viljoen Game Park	19	Mudumu & Mamili	46
Swakopmund	20	Khaudum Game Reserve	48
Walvis Bay	22	Waterberg Plateau Park	49
Lüderitz	24	Hardap & Lüderitz Peninsula	50
Sesfontein & Opuwo	25	Kolmanskop	51
Oshakati & Rundu	26		
Katima Mulilo & Tsumeb	27	**TOURING / DRIVING MAPS**	**52**
Grootfontein & Otavi	28		
Outjo & Otjiwarongo	29	**INDEX**	**91**
Omaruru & Henties Bay	30		
Okahandja & Gobabis	31	**RESOURCES**	**94**
Rehoboth & Mariental	32		
Keetmanshoop	33		

Introduction Introduction Introdu

Introduction

Namibia, land of shifting sand, is a rough diamond on the African coast waiting to be cut and polished by any eager travellers making their way through this vast land. The treacherous Skeleton Coast lures you in, while Sossusvlei's giant waves of red sand mystify you, along with the numerous ghost towns (the social scrapyards of past glories in the world of diamond mining), drawing you ever closer with the promise of stories untold. There's wildlife in abundance and some of the natural world's most breathtaking landscapes, dramatic vistas and awe-inspiring caves to explore, although the Fish River Canyon must take pride of place as one of the world's great natural wonders. Some of the most desired national parks on the continent beckon the traveller, who'll usually be welcomed with open arms by the sub-2-million population who inhabit this ancient land, among them the legendary Bushmen who still sail barefoot across Namibia's great seas of sand. People come to Namibia to lose themselves yet, lost in all this space, many instead succeed only in finding themselves.

"If your mouth turns into a knife, it will cut off your lips."
"The trees never meet (but people do)." – Namibian proverbs.

Historical Historical Historical His

A LONG, LONG TIME AGO …
Evidence of Stone Age occupation of Namibia exists in rock paintings estimated to be 25,000 years or older. Centuries later various groups of Bushmen (San hunter-gatherers) wandered in and settled parts of this vast expanse of land, and later Khoikhoi (the ancestors of the Nama), Bantu-speaking tribes, Hereros, Basters and Owambos made their home in Namibia.

TAKE ME TO YOUR LEADER
Namibia's long history is of human courage, African tribal migration, settlement and conflict, a position as a strategic military stronghold along the African coastline, colonial exploration and exploitation by Britain, Germany and South Africa. UN-supervised elections were held in November 1989 and Namibia became independant on 21 March 1990. Independence and a period of blissful co-existence brought every promise for a bright future, despite some minor political instability and sporadic acts of violence. Almost four times the size of Great Britain, Namibia is one of Africa's most sparsely populated countries, largely owing to the arid nature of this low-rainfall area.

COMINGS AND GOINGS
The 1480s were a busy time along Namibia's coast as first Diego Cāo (a Portuguese navigator) planted a stone cross (padrão) at Cape Cross in 1486 (roughly 130km north of Swakopmund), followed two years later by Bartolomeu Dias at present-day Lüderitz (then Angra Pequena, or Little Bay). The spot where Dias erected his cross was appropriately named Dias Point. Considering the proliferation of British, German and Portuguese influences on Southern Africa, it's ironic that a Swedish adventurer and

Cormorants nesting on a wrecked ship on the treacherous Skeleton Coast. Many a ship has run aground on this bitter coastline.

explorer (named Charles John Andersson) should coin the name South West Africa in his travel journal, a name which stuck, albeit with the somewhat temporary adjustment to German South West Africa, when Otto von Bismarck proclaimed the country a German protectorate in 1884).
Neighbouring South Africa sent forces in to overthrow the Germans during World War I, and thus brought the territory under their administration after the War. In 1966 SWAPO (the South West African People's Organisation) took up arms against the occupying forces of their 'rulers', and after much fighting and years of strife, free and fair elections were arranged following the implementation of United Nations Resolution 435 in 1989. SWAPO won at the polls that same year, thus signalling independence for the land after more than a century of foreign rule. Long-time advocate for independence, Dr Sam Nujoma, became his country's first president, and remained in office till 2005 and was succeeded by Hifikepunye Pohamba.

Bushman rock paintings at Twyfelfontein.

> "The earth is not ours, it is a treasure we hold in trust for future generations."
> Old African proverb.

Historical

DIVIDE AND RULE
After independence Namibia was divided into 13 regions: the north comprised Omusati, Oshana, Ohangwena and Oshikoto; the Kunene lies in the north-west; Kavango and Caprivi in the north-east; the central part is made up of Erongo, Otjozondjupa, Omaheke, Khomas and Hardap; and, finally, there is Karas in the south.

Namibia's democratic constitution is highly regarded by the international community, and the country is ruled by a multiparty parliament, with the overriding policy of national reconciliation and unity striving to embrace the noble concepts of tolerance and respect for differing political views, as well as racial and ethnic harmony. Power is divided between the executive, the legislature and the judiciary under the constitution.

THE ART OF DIPLOMACY
Namibia hosts the following diplomatic missions: Algeria, Angola, Botswana, Brazil, China, Congo, Cuba, Egypt, the European Union, Finland, France, Germany, Ghana, India, Indonesia, Italy, Kenya, Libya, Malawi, Malaysia, Mexico, the Netherlands, Nigeria, Portugal, the Russian Federation, South Africa, Spain, Sweden, Great Britain and Ireland, the United States of America, Venezuela, Zambia and Zimbabwe.

LANGUAGES
English is the official language, but with numerous different tribes as well as colonial influences, it's hardly surprising to find a multitude of languages spoken throughout Namibia. Bantu languages are spoken by the Owambo, Herero, Kavango, Caprivians and Tswana; the descendants of colonial explorers and masters speak one or more of Afrikaans, German and English (although many Namibians can communicate in one or more of these three languages); and Khoisan languages are spoken by the Bushmen (or San), Nama and Damara people.

POPULATION
Based on figures from the official 2001 census, Namibia's population swelled by over 400,000 people during the previous decade, reaching a high of more than 1,800,000 people. Interestingly, there are 50,000 more women than men. The most densely populated region is the Khomas (which includes Windhoek), with over a quarter of a million people, little more than a 100 'head' ahead of Ohangwena. The Kavango region occupies third spot, lagging 50,000 'heads' behind. Unfortunately, it's not a good country for individuals who suffer from agoraphobia (fear of open spaces), as Namibia enjoys one of the world's lowest population densities – on average there are less than two people per square kilometre.

Namibia's ghost towns offer a window back into the country's diamond mining boom days. Bogenfels (top) and Kolmanskop (left) are both popular tourist attractions.

Namibians work in many different fields, ranging from the hunter-gatherers to formal farmers, in addition to a highly-skilled and diverse urban population.

People People People People Peo

Himba women boast refined features, elaborate hairstyles and traditional adornments.

Herero women wear distinctive Victorian-style dresses and interesting headwear.

THE CAPRIVIANS number around 80,000 and live in the Caprivi Strip. They are mostly subsistence farmers who make their living from cultivating crops, keeping cattle and fishing. These resourceful people are adaptable to the seasons: those living on the eastern floodplains of the Zambezi and Chobe rivers move seasonally, depending on the level of the floods.

Namibia's COLOURED community, along with the Basters, hails from the Cape Province in South Africa: both speak Afrikaans as their home language, although with different accents and dialects. Many are fishermen who ply the waters around Walvis Bay for their livelihood, while there are a large number of well educated coloureds, many of whom enjoy professional employment.

THE DAMARA are proud to be one of the country's oldest cultural groups, and from their ranks come many politicians who are among the most eloquent in Namibia's parliament. Their traditional homeland, Damaraland, was renamed the Erongo Region after independence in 1990, with a population numbering over 100,000.

THE HERERO migrated to Namibia centuries ago. They suffered great population losses during the colonial wars and in the 1904/5 Herero Uprising. Pastoral cattle breeders, they have retained their bonds of family life and tribal solidarity despite the wartime losses and proudly celebrate their national consciousness with a festival on Maherero Day in Okahandja every August, which includes a display of military pomp through the town's streets.

THE HIMBA are a semi-nomadic tribe of pastoralists based in the Kunene region. They live in cone-shaped 'homes' made from saplings, palm leaves, mud and dung. Proud yet friendly, these famously beautiful people are tall, slender and statuesque. They adorn themselves with bracelets, anklets, necklaces, iron belts and beautiful beads made from shells. The women protect their skin from the harsh desert sun by coating their bodies with red ochre and fat.

The Kavango River provides a lifeline for THE KAVANGO people, whose numbers have swelled to over 200,000, causing 'domestic overcrowding': on average, six and a half people live in each household! Many of the younger generation are migratory farm labourers, miners and urban workers, while those who remain closer to home ply the Kavango for fish, cultivate crops on the surrounding fertile plains or tend their cattle.

Also known as the San, Namibia's hunter-gatherer BUSHMEN are around 35,000 strong in numbers and enjoy a proud tradition as great storytellers, musicians, mimics and dancers. Their forefathers wandered South Africa's plains for thousands of years, leaving a wealth of rock art and engravings (notably the White Lady painting found in the Brandberg, as well as Twyfelfontein, the bushmen's equivalent of the Louvre) to stake their claim as one of Namibia's oldest peoples. Some of their paintings date back almost 30,000 years. A large proportion of the Bushmen now live a 'normal' life in villages, while some continue to enjoy a traditional, nomadic existence (mostly in Botswana).

Great storytellers and poets, the Namas of the southern region find their language on the list of "Languages in Danger of Disappearing".

People People People People Peop

THE NAMA are Namibia's only pure Khoikhoi descendants. Certain distinctive characteristics, such as the women's small and slender hands and feet, make the Khoikhoi easily distinguishable. Nama have a natural talent for music, poetry and prose. An example of a traditional dance is the well-known Nama "stap". Numerous proverbs, riddles, tales and poems have been handed down orally from generation to generation. Nama women are highly skilled in sewing. Their embroidery and appliqué work, today regarded as a traditional art form, consists of brightly coloured motifs inspired by their rural environment and lifestyles. The content of their work is often expressive and humorous, as seen in the colourful, traditional patchwork dresses that the Nama women wear.

OWAMBO is a collective name for a number of tribes living in central northern Namibia and southern Angola. Of the nine Owambo tribes, the Kwanyama group is the largest. The most striking feature of the traditional Owambo social system is the predominance of matrilineal descent, which determines the laws of inheritance and succession, as well as post-marital residency. As a result of external factors such as the Christian doctrine, migrant labour and economic independence, there has been a distinct shift towards a patrilineally organized society.

THE REHOBOTH BASTERS can trace their roots back to the day Jan van Riebeeck's settlers first set foot at the Cape of Good Hope in South Africa. The children that resulted from the meetings of the European settlers and the Khoisan were branded "Coloureds" or "Bastards". In 1868 almost 100 Baster families migrated to Namibia, ultimately putting down roots at the hot-water springs called Rehoboth. Today the Baster community consists of approximately 72,000 people. Their mother tongue is Afrikaans and, at their own request, they have been registered as Rehoboth Basters. The Basters regard themselves as a separate community from the Coloureds by virtue of their unique history and the fact that they have been living in their own territory for more than a century.

THE TOPNAARS are a hardy people of Nama origin who have lived on the banks of the Kuiseb River for many years. Belonging to the Khoikhoi people, they speak the Nama language with its guttural clicks and high musical pitch. Central to their culinary tradition is the *!nara* melon, a large and nutritious fruit which is endemic to the Namib. The *!nara* melon is believed to enjoy certain medicinal properties.

An elderly Nama man in Keetmanshoop enjoying his pipe, perhaps while trying to solve one of the many age-old Nama riddles.

THE TSWANA are Namibia's smallest cultural group, numbering around a mere 8,000. Namibia's rural Tswana live in The Corridor, a narrow strip along the border with Botswana, where they are involved in cattle farming. Many of them have bought commercial farms in the Gobabis district.

THE WHITES (descended from European stock and almost all urban-dwellers and farmers) number around 100,000 of Namibia's population, and the majority are Afrikaans-speaking, with German- and English-speakers making up the rest. Roughly 150 Portuguese families (originally from Angola) still call Namibia home.

Kids in the Caprivi area take a moment to smile for the camera, despite the pain of a broken arm.

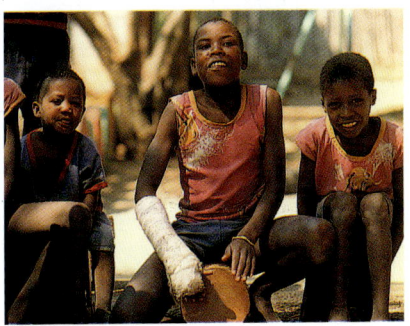

9

"It never rains, but it pours" seems to sum up Namibia's unreliable rainfall patterns over much of the country for much of the year.

Nature Nature Nature Nature Nat

The greater kestrel is able to hover in the air as it watches the ground beneath it for prey.

THE SIZE OF IT
Namibia covers an area of almost 825,000 km², in parts as wide as 1,440km and in others as narrow as 350km. You'd need more than 5,700km of measuring tape to accurately measure its perimeter; over 1,500km is coastline (from the mouth of the Cunene down to the Orange River mouth). Namibia also controls an exclusive economic zone of some 200 nautical miles off its coast, which amounts to well over half a million square kilometres of ocean.

QUITE A RELIEF
A large portion of Namibia consists of a wide open plateau that spills into neighbouring countries at altitudes of between 900m and 1,300m. In parts massive escarpments jutt up from around the coast, the incisions were created over centuries by geological processes as well as the effects of erosion caused by vast river systems, for example in the Fish River Canyon. Aside from becoming president, the highest point a Namibian can reach is by climbing the 2,579m high Brandberg ('burnt mountain'). Namibia offers geologists endless pleasures, not least because so many of its spectacular rock formations are so beautifully exposed. Notable among these are the granite hills of the Spitzkoppe, which are remnants of great masses of magma that were forced into the earth's crust around 130 million years ago when the Gondwana supercontinent started breaking up to separate Namibia from South America.

BEAUTIFUL BIRDS
Well over 600 species of bird have been recorded (11 endemic), with around 500 breeding in Namibia. Notable endemic species include the Herero chat, Monteiro's hornbill, Damara tern, rockrunner, long-toed plover and the greater swamp warbler. The majestic African Fish Eagle is found near water (as well as on the country's coat of arms), while the sociable weaver will enchant birdwatchers with its amazing system of communal nests – which it constructs in trees or on telephone poles – that can house hundreds of birds (some nests have survived for many decades). The brightly coloured malachite kingfisher, with its short tail and relatively long, red beak, is one of hundreds of species that grace the waters of the Caprivi region.

Left: *Two beetles scurry along the desert sand.*
Right: *An armoured ground cricket.*

Elephants enjoying a drink at a local waterhole.

AN ABUNDANCE OF WILDLIFE
Namibia enjoys a glorious wildlife population, with numerous species of game throughout the country, including eight endemic species of mammal (among them the black-faced impala, various mice, gerbils and bats). The big game includes leopard, lion and cheetah, in addition to elephant, rhino (white and black), hippopotamus and giraffe, as well as buffalo, Burchell's zebra and Hartmann's mountain zebra. The numerous species of antelope include eland, the greater kudu, roan and sable antelope, gemsbok, wildebeest, waterbuck, lechwe, sitatunga, red hartbeest, nyala, springbuck, impala, reedbuck, oribi, bushbuck and the

The long-horned gemsbok can survive for long periods without water and can endure temperatures greater than 45 °C.

Nature Nature Nature Nature Nat

5kg Damara dik-dik, which only stands up to 40cm high on its stick-like legs. Jackals, hyaena, wild dogs and warthogs will also put in an appearance on many a wildlife expedition, as well as dassies (rock hyrax), chacma baboons and vervet monkeys. The harsh landscape naturally limits the variety and abundance of wildlife to some extent, yet equally it provides the perfect survival conditions for a number of endemic animals. The Namib desert boasts a wide range of *toktokkies* (tenebrionids) and other beetles (such as the 'fog-trapping' beetle), as well as lizards (Skoog's lizard burrows to safety in the sand with a unique corkscrew motion) and a wide range of other interesting insects and reptiles.

HARD-HEADED FLORA
Namibia's dramatically different climates (from the coast to the harsh interior) create an environment that caters for a wide range of plant life, although the land is best known for its hardier species which have overcome the elements to thrive. Most famous is probably the endemic Welwitschia of the Namib desert, which can live from 500 to 2,000 years, one of the oldest known plants in the world. There are more than 120 tree species, including the umbrella-shaped camel thorn, the baobab, quiver trees (or kokerboom), marula, paper bark trees, mopane, figs, leadwood, jackalsbessie, Boesmangif (bushman's poison) and Makalani palms. Other plant life includes reeds and palms on the floodplains and the common driedoring flower (three-thorned flower). A fascinating array of lichens (there are more than 100 kinds throughout Namibia, some of which are endemic) can be found in the desert – these rely totally on moisture from the coastal fog for their survival. In all, Namibia has more than 200 endemic plant species, including the lithops (commonly known as the flowering stones). Other well-known plants include the *halfmens*, the elephant's foot and a number of dwarf succulents which are found near Lüderitz.

Top: *Flowering lithops.*
Above: *The welwitschia is an ancient plant of the Namib region that can live for more than a thousand years ... yet in all that time it will produce only two leaves.*

Bushmen once used the unusual hollow branches of the quiver tree (kokerboom) as quivers to hold their arrows.

Namibia's dramatic and treacherous terrain promises modern explorers stiff challenges and unforgettable adventures.

Activities Activities Activities Act

SAND'S UP
Namibia's coastal dunes provide endless enjoyment for visitors, and are one of the best places in the world to enjoy sand skiing and sand-boarding – the idea is to push off the top of a dune and lie on the board as it slides down. Speeds easily reach 70kph. Dune-boarding may seem more refined, but it requires more skill to stand up on a small surfboard as it shoots down the side of a dune. Quadbiking involves riding 4-wheel motorcycles over and around the dunes. Though these organized trips are well regulated, the reckless use of quad bikes is increasingly damaging the fragile environment, and harming the coastal wildlife.

SADDLE UP
Namibia has perfect conditions for horse riding, with routes crossing mountains, bush and wooded areas to desert plains and dunes. Alternatively, for a more Arabian experience, camel riding is available in places along the coast. For something completely different, and authentically Namibian, try an exciting donkey-cart drive, the traditional transport of the Topnaar people.

TAKE THE PLUNGE
Adding an exhilarating dimension to a visit to the Namib desert is a trip in a hot-air balloon. For those individuals who enjoy taking their lives into their own hands and having adrenaline pumping through their veins, skydiving over land and sea is the answer. Paragliding enthusiasts occasionally undertake powered paragliding excursions along the coast.

Top: *4WD trips through the desert sands might seem like a ticket to ride wild, but respect for the environment and caution for your personal safety should be uppermost in your mind.*
Above: *Desert hikes are one of the ultimate human tests against the elements.*

OVER WATER
White-water canoeing has taken off in a big way on the Cunene River, but it's advisable to join a tour offered by an experienced adventure company if you're not experienced. Between Ruacana and Epupa there are rapids at Ondorusu and Enyandi, while Epupa Falls is set in scenic surroundings and is blessed with interesting vegetation and bird life. Canoeing safaris are offered down the Orange River, departing from Noordoewer or Aussenkehr and ending at Aussenkehr or the Fish River mouth respectively.

UNDER WATER
Dragon's Breath Cave (on Harasib farm) lays claim to the world's largest known subterranean lake. To explore it you will need valid cave diving gear and qualifications and more courage than the average person. Harasib Cave and Lake are reached through an opening found on Ghaub Mountain, and both are worth exploring. The lake has an amazing natural display of stalactites and stalagmites. Lying 24km away from Tsumeb is the 76m

Quadbiking on Namibia's dunes is an increasingly popular pursuit and there are outlets between Swakopmund and Walvis Bay.

Namibia offers a wide range of activities, from sedate family trips to high-adrenaline, blood-curdling adventures requiring great skill and courage.

Activities

deep Lake Otjikoto (also only for qualified divers) which will yield a treasure trove of abandoned weapons and armaments dumped here after World War I: great wreck diving for the experienced diver. On the whole, Namibia's coast presents tough conditions for scuba divers, with visibility ranging from half a metre up to usually no more than four metres. To add to the visual difficulty, temperatures in these waters range from 9°C to 17°C.

CASTING YOUR LINE
Aspects that make coastal angling from the beach especially enjoyable are the peaceful desert environments and the uncrowded beaches. Namibia's dams in the interior offer several options for those wishing to try their hand at freshwater angling. The far eastern tip of the Caprivi, at the confluence of the Chobe and Zambezi rivers, is regarded as a tiger fishing paradise second to none.

Sunset fishing on an uncrowded beach, with the desert sands behind you, will help clear the mental cobwebs from most city slickers' heads.

HUNTING
Namibia's abundant wildlife attracts hunting enthusiasts from afar to partake in trophy and safari hunting, bird hunting, as well as the ancient art of bow hunting. Written permission must be obtained from the farmer whose land your hunting party intends using before the authorities will issue a hunting permit. Note that the official term 'huntable game' strictly excludes any protected animals.

FOUR–WHEEL DRIVE
There are countless four-wheel drive opportunities in this sandy and rocky landscape, both supervised and unsupervised. Some of the more popular and challenging include: the Dorsland Trek 4x4 Route, Isabis 4x4 Trail, Saddle Hill, Topnaar 4x4 Trail, Conception Bay Route and the Naukluft Route.

TAKE A HIKE
Owing to high summer temperatures, tough terrain and scarcity of water, hiking in Namibia requires careful planning. Hiking is not advisable in the summer months when temperatures often exceed 40°C. Some of the best destinations and trails include: the Fish River Canyon (one of Southern Africa's top five), the Naukluft Hiking Trail, the Ugab River Hiking Trail (in the south of the Skeleton Coast Park), the Dassie Trails Network, the Sweet Thorn Hiking Trail, the Tok Tokkie Trails, the Waterberg Hiking Trail and the Waterberg Wilderness Trail.

MOUNTAINEERING & ROCK CLIMBING
Spitzkoppe's vast granite dome rises about 700m above the desert plains between Windhoek and Swakopmund. Also referred to as Namibia's Matterhorn, the Spitzkoppe – with its almost perpendicular slopes – is one of the great mountaineering opportunities in Africa. Brandberg is a sought-after area for both mountaineers and backpackers. Due to the extremely rugged terrain and limited water, excursions should only be undertaken by experienced and fit backpackers. Abseiling is also gaining popularity due to some of Namibia's spectacular rock formations.

Hot air balloon rides offer visitors spectacular views of the Namibian landscape.

Towns Towns Towns Towns Towns

Most travel guides promise that Namibia's towns (especially the "small little holes in the ground" out in the middle of nowhere) are good merely for stopping, stretching and stocking up on petrol and some niceties. Of course, it all depends how you look at it and what you're looking for! You won't find the CRASH-BOOM-BANG sights and sounds that draw the horrible hordes to the junk-food destinations. Thank your lucky stars: that's not what makes Namibia unique. The towns speak of a heritage shared across cultures and oceans, and there's no rush here: nothing is going to dash off before you get to it. If you tune into Namibia's frequency her beauty will go bang...crash...boom in tiny ripples through your soul. Drift. Wander around small museums in tiny towns. Take 10 minutes to look at the quaint memorials to bygone heroes. Ask the locals about the weather, and the best place to make a braai. This is not an 'instant' holiday spot, it's an adventure waiting to be lived.

Namibia's capital is a modern, vibrant African city whose high-rises and pedestrian shopping malls speak of prosperity and progress.

Windhoek Windhoek Windhoek

Located 1,500m above sea level, Windhoek sits sheltered by the Eros Mountains (slightly north) and the Aus Mountains (south of the capital).

Windhoek Windhoek Wind

With an average of 1mm of rain a day, Windhoek's population of just over 200,000 no doubt primarily use their umbrellas for sun protection.

Windhoek Windhoek Windhoek W

Relaxed, yet alive with people and an array of vibrant cultures, Windhoek gives the visitor a generous feeling of welcome without engulfing them like a typical western capital. Despite its large proportion of indigenous inhabitants, the concrete face of Windhoek is very German in nature, the architecture and numerous war memorials paying homage to the former colonial masters.

Windhoek has a reasonable entertainment infrastructure, with well attended and popular nightclubs, bars and restaurants. For visitors or locals seeking engagements of a more cerebral nature, there are art galleries and museums that boast impressive exhibits, as well as a theatre and a cinema (with five screens). If you're architecturally inclined you'll be able to amuse yourself for hours in Windhoek, which boasts a rich tradition of colonial German buildings in addition to newer post-modernist constructions. And, of course, the three castles on the hills (all completed by 1917) overlooking the city centre provide further fascination. Heinitzburg, the second to be built, is now an upmarket hotel and a good spot for sundowners.

WHERE THE STREETS HAVE FAMOUS NAMES
A walk down Independence Avenue will offer views of some stunning German colonial architecture, the Clock Tower, Zoo Park's lawns and palm trees, the Curt von Francois statue, and the Augustino Neto Gardens. You'll also notice some famous road names: Sam Nujoma Drive, Robert Mugabe Avenue and Nelson Mandela Drive.

THE RIDER MEMORIAL
An enormous statue stands at the entrance to the Alte Feste (Old Fort), Windhoek's oldest surviving building, and now the National Museum of Namibia. The statue – Reiter Denkmal (the Rider Memorial) – depicts a larger-than-life but typical German Protection Force soldier. The statue was erected in memory of the *Schutztruppe* (German soldiers) who died during the 1903-1907 wars against the Herero and Nama.

LOOK AT THIS
Post Street Mall boasts the largest display of meteorites in the world – or so say the locals – 33 making up a sculpture in the middle of the Mall! The Gibeon meteorites rained down on earth probably 600 million years ago, over 20 tons of rock (77 meteorites in all) having been collected in the area around Gibeon, near Mariental.

Windhoek city walk.

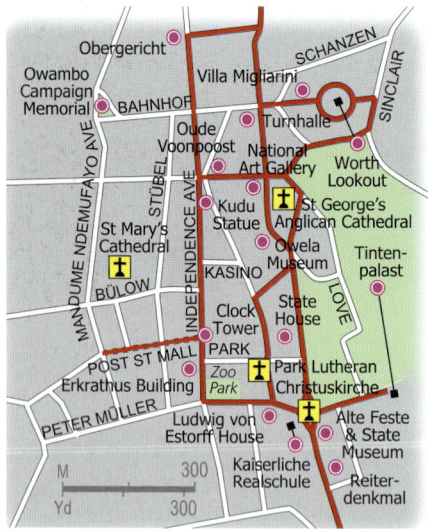

The Rider Memorial.

18

In 1959 Windhoek's black population was forcibly removed to Katutura, which is Herero for "we have no dwelling place".

hoek Windhoek Windhoek Windh

ALOE-ALOE
The aloe – a hardy plant with large, fleshy leaves for storing water in arid conditions – is an icon of Namibia. Aloes usually present themselves in a stunning winter display around town, but they can also be appreciated in the Windhoek Botanical Gardens.

DAAN VILJOEN GAME PARK
Close to Windhoek, Daan Viljoen Game Park is equipped for travellers and offers driving opportunities for standard cars. The park has three main trails: Wag-'n-Bietjie (Buffalo-thorn) Trail, Rooibos (bushwillow) Trail and Sweet-Thorn Trail. It offers good game spotting and has a prolific birdlife (including the Damara rockjumper and the rosy-faced lovebird). Walking is relatively safe as four of the Big Five (and dangerous) don't inhabit the Park (lion, elephant, rhino and buffalo).

Christuskirche, Windhoek's Evangelical Lutheran church, consecrated in 1910.

Top Tip
For hikers, the purchase of *Birds of Daan Viljoen* (from the parks office), will be money well spent: it has a checklist of bird species as well as other useful information on the birds and the park.

19

Namibia's holiday mecca, Swakop (as the locals call it) offers lovely beaches for anglers, surfers, bathers and sun-worshippers to share.

Swakopmund Swakopmund Swa

Swakop is small enough to be explored on foot, and interesting enough to make the effort worthwhile. It's also the adventure and activity centre of Namibia (which includes parachuting, sand-boarding and dune-bike riding) and as such it's little surprise that the town is extremely tourist friendly, while maintaining the ability to slip back into sleepy-hollow mode at certain times of the week, month or year. There are plenty of cultural attractions (libraries, museums, commercial art galleries, curio stores and interesting buildings) to occupy the non-adrenaline junkie.

Swakopmund Prison, often mistaken by visitors for a hotel.

Top Tip
The Sam Cohen Library has 7,000 volumes of Africana books and literature on Swakopmund, as well as old photos, maps and German and English newspapers dating back to 1898.

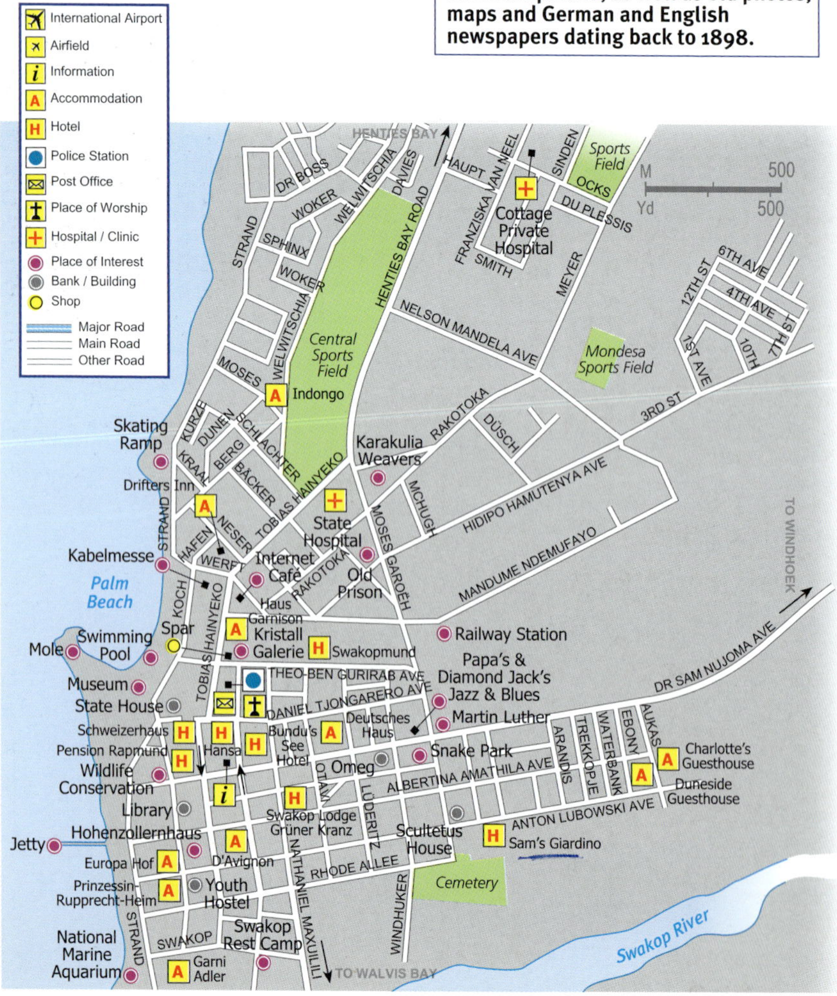

20

English is Namibia's official language, but German is widely used ... and Swakop residents in particular are well-versed in the language.

Swakopmund

RUNNING OUT OF STEAM
One of Swakop's most famous pieces of history lies just outside of town – nicknamed 'Martin Luther', the now rusty old steam engine was imported from Hamburg in Germany to take the place of oxen who struggled in the heat.

NATIONAL MARINE AQUARIUM
Hand-feeding by divers, an underwater walkway through the huge main tank and a wide array of local marine life (ranging from sharks to crayfish) make Swakop's aquarium a good place to spend half an hour or longer.

Swakopmund walk.

SWAKOP RIVER DELTA
A couple of hundred metres from the Aquarium is the Swakop River Delta, an excellent spot for birdwatching and bird photography (including flamingo, pelican, cormorants and kestrels) with a 4km river trail for walkers.

Top Trip
A short drive out of town are sand dunes that are ideal for adventure sports (4x4, sand dune boarding, quadbiking) as well as the Welwitschia Drive in the Namib-Naukluft Park.

The old jetty, originally built in 1911 during the German colonial era.

THE ABOMINABLE JETTY
Swakop's well-known iron jetty stretches 262m into the ocean but is now unfortunately dilapidated, has been closed to the public and exists merely as a landmark rather than a tourist 'attraction'. The lighthouse can be seen from as far as 30km away – a good thing considering how treacherous Namibia's Skeleton Coast has been over the last century.

HARBOURING NO BAD FEELINGS
Swakop was founded by the Germans in 1892 in order to match the British who had already established their own 'port presence' at Walvis Bay on the strategically valuable Skeleton Coast. Sadly, Swakop proved a poor choice, as the harbour was prone to silting up. Just 14 years later the government hoped the construction of a mole would help to create an artificial harbour that could function properly. Regrettably, sandbanks built up and ruined any chance for the harbour. On a more positive note, it did improve the safety and bathing pleasure for beach users and the mole is now used as a launching spot for boats and small craft. It also allows walkers the chance to see dolphins at close range.

Swakopmund is a good base for visiting the dramatic Spitzkoppe, which are just over 100km away from town.

21

Walvis Bay's huge saltwater lagoon is a vital habitat for flamingoes who flock there in their thousands all year round.

Walvis Bay Walvis Bay Walvis Ba

The long, straight and rolling road between Walvis Bay and Swakopmund.

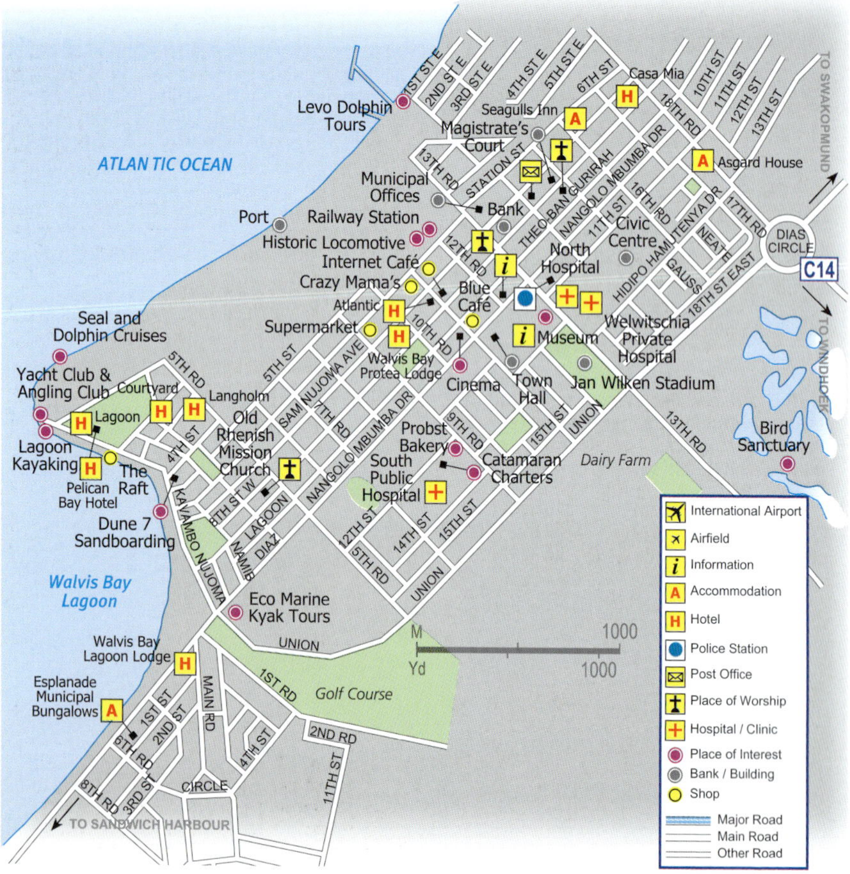

Namibia's best natural harbour (and only deepwater port), Walvis is a vital base for patrolling the valuable fishing ground and offshore diamond fields.

alvis Bay Walvis Bay Walvis Bay

Walvis Bay lies 30km south of Swakopmund, and many visitors stay in Swakop and journey down to Walvis to partake in the birdwatching (numerous seabirds, including the favourite flamingoes and pelicans), angling, seal-spotting cruises offshore (if you're in luck you'll get to see dolphin and even sunfish from your craft), or the more leisurely boating activities on the lagoon. The architecture of the town lacks the character of Swakop's German charm, possibly because the port was annexed by the British in 1878 (the Germans never took control of Walvis and were forced to lay port elsewhere).

Top: *Greater flamingoes in flight.*
Above: *Pelican preening itself.*

Top Trip
Avoid the tourist trap of activities centred solely on the lagoon – explore some of the magnificent desert sights and scenery that surrounds the town. It's an experience largely untapped by visitors.

The legendary Bartolomeu Dias is down in the history books as the first European to visit here, back in 1487, and he named the spot Bay of Whales. For the next two centuries whalers and numerous other vessels dropped anchor in Walvis Bay (as well as at Sandwich Harbour), and when the Dutch came to town in 1793 they adapted its name to Walvisbaai (Walvis Bay), and some claim their influence is still felt in the town's lack of architectural character! Walvis' small population of just over 40,000 rely on fish and fishing for their livelihood as well as salt production (Walvis supplies more than 90% of South Africa's salt. The salt is evaporated from seawater trapped in a 3,500-hectare 'salt pan'. Tours of the salt works are offered by local tour operators. Walvis Bay Lagoon is one of the two most valuable wetland areas (along with the nearby Sandwich Harbour) to be found throughout the entire West coast of Africa. The lagoon is able to support more than 150,000 birds in summer and almost 70,000 in winter, notably the greater and lesser flamingoes, pelicans, migrant waders and seabirds. Wait for low-tide to get your best birding opportunities as the birds scour the shallow water for tasty marine morsels.

A good catch, a quiet beach, and a friend to bear witness to your success. Fisherman's paradise!

Top Tip
For a different experience, stop by the Raft Restaurant (built on stilts in the Walvis Bay lagoon) and enjoy a bite to eat or a drink at the bar. It's 'a good place to be seen'!

The unusual pastel shades of many of the houses in this laid-back but character-rich town have led some to playfully call it 'Ludicrous'.

Lüderitz Lüderitz Lüderitz Lüderitz

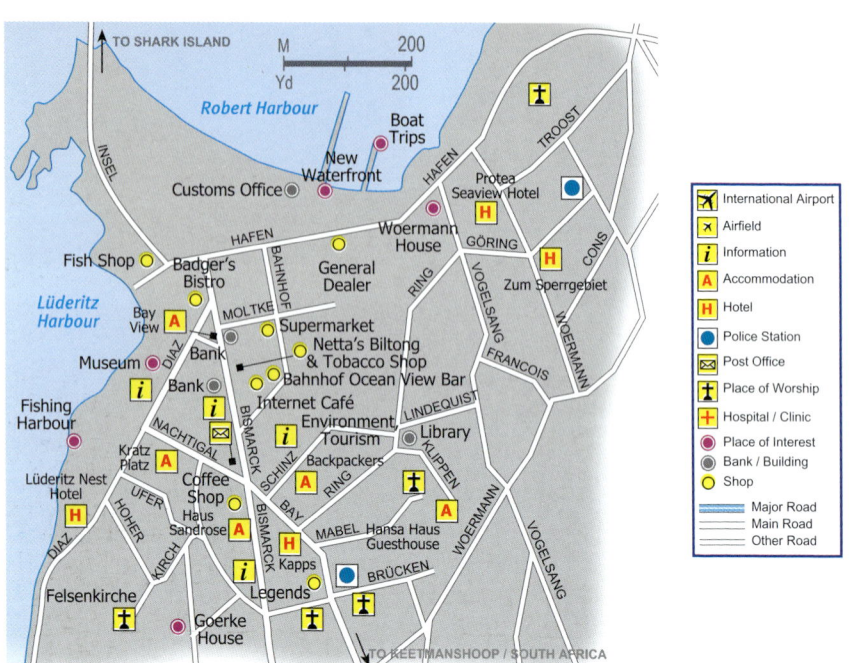

Top Tip: Plan your wardrobe carefully: Lüderitz's weather is 'predictably unpredictable'. Within a few hours Mother Nature might hurl sunshine, fog, cold, wind and even rain at you. Locals 'joke' that the wind is so strong it blasts the paint off cars. Joke?

Some of Lüderitz's brightly coloured buildings.

A favourite travel destination and a stunning example of friendly, small-town and slow-paced hospitality, rich in German tradition and history, Lüderitz is worth the effort to visit for a few days. Sitting more than 360km from Keetmanshoop, Lüderitz is literally and figuratively isolated from the rest of the world. However, it's not cut off completely, as it has a rich supply of public telephones that seem to pop up on every corner. Tourism is increasing and accommodation options are happily opening up to meet the new demand, with the first phase of a new waterfront development already completed. Part of Lüderitz's charm is that its isolation for so many years has left the town with a wealth of original architecture and interesting buildings from the 1900s. Added to this is the fun nature of the town, with its eccentric house colours and the midday siren that doubles-up as a fire alarm! Bartolomeu Dias also made his mark here and named the town Angra Pequena (Little Bay). A number of tools and artefacts dating back to the stone-age confirm that the Khoisan found 'Little Bay' some time before Dias! Kolmanskop and Elizabeth Bay ghost towns are a comfortable drive from Lüderitz and are both worth the effort.

Named after the six springs (ses fontein) found here, this dusty little town in the middle of nowhere lies central to all the delights of northwest Namibia.

Sesfontein Opuwo Sesfontein Opuw

SESFONTEIN ▼

Fort Sesfontein was established as a German army outpost to keep an eye on the area militarily as well as from a crime and gun-running perspective prior to World War I. Abandoned and in an awful state of deterioration for decades, it was given a facelift and general overhaul and converted into a comfy oasis-like lodge. It's an ideal base for explorations into the surrounding Kaokoland and Damaraland. The historic graveyard is worth a wander. Take in the views of the town and its mountain backdrop from the shale and limestone hills that skirt the fort.

A wall of tins built by the locals in Opuwo.

Opuwo made its name as a base used by the South African troops during times of conflict and occupation in Namibia. It is an otherwise unpretentious little settlement lost in the bush and tucked away in its own small 'crater', although there are some interesting local dwellings, such as traditional rondavels (round huts) and Himba huts. Opuwo has two 'supermarkets' and a fish shop called Madiba (Nelson Mandela's nickname).

About 29km out of town is Ongongo Camp, which means 'beautiful little place', and the Blinkwater Falls back up this claim. Otjitaimo Canyon is 10km out of town and is hard to reach on foot, yet it offers rich rewards for seekers of solitude and spectacular scenery.

Top Tip: Locals will be willing to act as guides to the town (for a fee), but they no longer think tourist cameras are worth a free smile. Be careful when encroaching on tribal land and always seek permission.

Top Trip: A day trip along the Hoanib River from Sesfontein to Purros offers great viewing of the desert elephant as well as numerous other forms of wildlife. Please note that it is advisable to travel with a guide.

OPUWO ▶

Opuwo means 'the end' in the native Herero tongue, which is fitting as it is a vital stocking-up point for travellers passing through … and passing through is what most people do in Opuwo, apart from using it as a base for exploring the surrounding area, which includes some nearby settlements of Himba and Herero people. Kaokoveld adventurers and explorers often use Opuwo as a stop-off point, or stop relatively near by.

25

Rundu presents weary Caprivi-bound travellers with a relative oasis to wash away the bleak desert landscape through which they have travelled.

Oshakati Rundu Oshakati Rundu

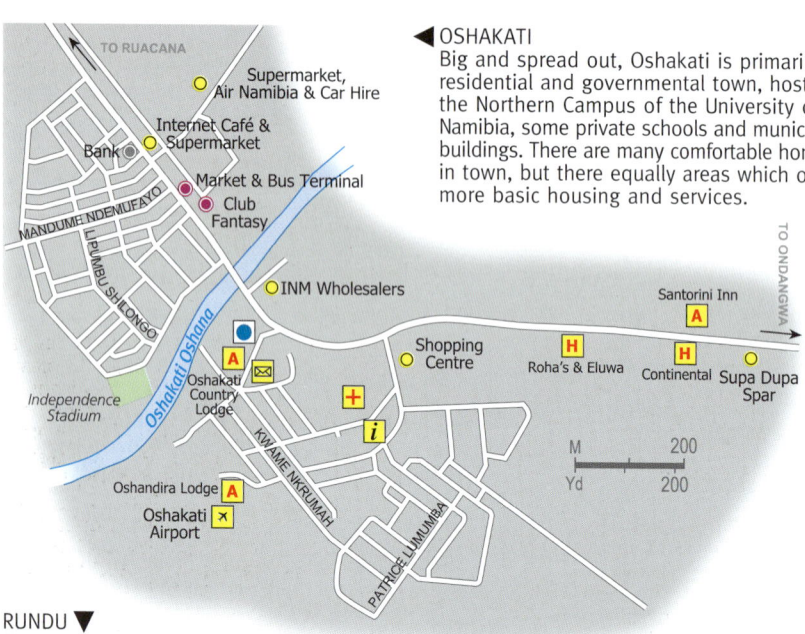

◀ OSHAKATI
Big and spread out, Oshakati is primarily a residential and governmental town, hosting the Northern Campus of the University of Namibia, some private schools and municipal buildings. There are many comfortable homes in town, but there equally areas which offer more basic housing and services.

RUNDU ▼
Situated above the Kavango (Okavango in Botswana) River floodplain, Rundu is a fabulous stopover en route to more entertaining and enjoyable activities or destinations, in the Kavango and Caprivi regions. Its proximity to Angola has given the little outpost of Rundu a Portuguese flavour mixed with a languid sense of calm. There are great views across the Kavango River, with some watersports, fishing and four-wheel drive opportunities for the energetic. Rundu is an important refueling stop for travellers: petrol is scarce in the area, and the town's bottle stores present shoppers with a fantastic array of products. Souvenir hunters will enjoy Rundu's happy hunting grounds: woodcarving in the area has a proud tradition.

Top Tip: Oshakati offers the potential of a big night out in a small town. Basic but welcoming, favourite spots include Club Fantasy (proclaiming itself to be 'your party place'), Let's Push Bar, Club Yellow Star and Moby Jack's.

Woodcarvings for sale in Rundu.

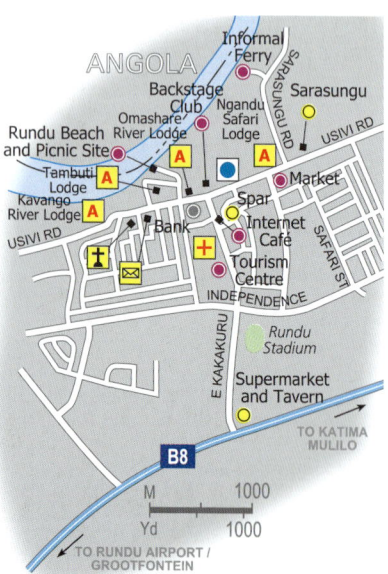

26

The patron saint of mine workers (believe it or not) is St Barbara ... and you'll find Tsumeb's St Barbara catholic church on Main Street.

Katima Mulilo Tsumeb

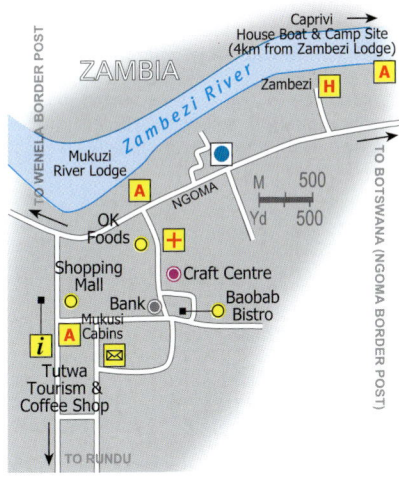

The mokoro (dug-out), a popular means of transport in the wetlands.

KATIMA MULILO ▲
Katima Mulilo boasts excellent facilities for travellers and is a great base for exploring as well as embarking on adventure activities. Located on the banks of the mighty Zambezi River, it provides an easy base from which to hop into Zambia, Zimbabwe or Botswana.

TSUMEB ▼
Tsumeb is attractive, with wide, quiet streets blessed with beautiful old colonial buildings and dressed with jacaranda, bougainvillea, palm trees, parks and lawns. Tsumeb's name can be translated to mean 'to dig a hole in loose ground', which is understandable given its status as one of Namibia's key mining towns. The crystals and gemstones unearthed here have earned the town a worldwide reputation. The Tsumeb Museum affords visitors a fantastic window into the past, while the Tsumeb Cultural Village is an open-air museum that allows visitors to glimpse first-hand what tribal life is all about in Namibia.

Top Sip
It's rough and ready for most big city folk; local eateries include The Butchy-Butchy Bakery (offering freshly baked bread) or you can rub shoulders with the local Crocodile Dundees at Mad Dog McGee's (a meat-eater's haven).

27

Otavi, Grootfontein and Tsumeb form the Maize Triangle, cultivating and providing much of Namibia's commercially grown maize.

Grootfontein Otavi Otavi Grootfo

GROOTFONTEIN ▼
Meaning 'large fountain' (there are strong natural springs in Tree Park), Grootfontein offers a pleasant stopover, as trees line the streets and limestone buildings stand proudly amid the spring explosions of jacaranda and red flamboyants.

Top Tip: A 2km drive out of Otavi will bring you to the Khorab Memorial. Erected in 1920, it marks the spot where the German forces capitulated to General Louis Botha's South African forces in 1915.

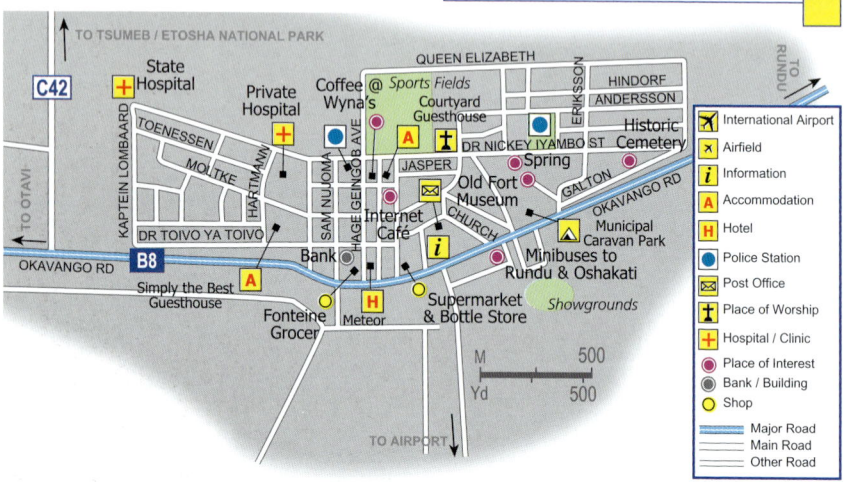

The enormous Hoba meteorite that landed near Grootfontein many thousands of years ago.

OTAVI ▼
Otavi's natural springs play a vital role in irrigating the surrounding farmlands, and it's no surprise that the name translates to 'place of water'. The town made its name during the copper-mining boom years at the turn of the century, and an amethyst mine is found just out of town.
Otavi hit the headlines with the 1991 discovery of the jawbone of a prehistoric ape-like creature dubbed the 'Otavi Ape', a creature which no doubt spent some time in the abundant caves in the area – anyone with an interest in caves will enjoy a great deal of time 'caving' themselves.

The fascinating Old Fort Museum (signposted as Die Alte Feste) off Eriksson Street has interesting historic photographs, gems, rocks and a display on the old art of wagon and cart manufacture. Straussen Ostrich Farm offers an insight into the ostrich industry, and includes a shop and a restaurant. The Hoba meteorite – the largest recorded meteorite on earth at around 60 tonnes – can be found 50km outside town. Almost three metres square (and between 75-122cm thick!), it may have celebrated in the region of 200 to 400 million birthdays, and it found its home here around 80,000 years ago.

Outjo means (appropriately) 'a place on the rocks', while Otjiwarongo was named by the Herero who thought of it as the 'place of the fat cattle'.

utjo Otjiwarongo Otjiwarongo Out

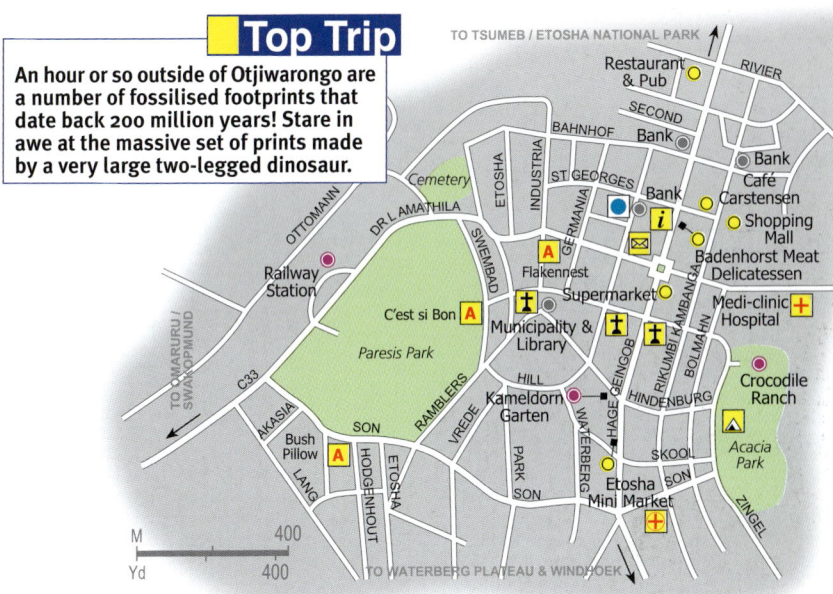

Top Trip
An hour or so outside of Otjiwarongo are a number of fossilised footprints that date back 200 million years! Stare in awe at the massive set of prints made by a very large two-legged dinosaur.

OTJIWARONGO ▲
Known for its spring explosions of jacaranda and bougainvillea, Otjiwarongo is situated close to the Waterberg Plateau Park. Otjiwarongo boasts Namibia's first crocodile ranch, which serves meals to visitors, sells meat to locals and exports skins to Asia. Look out for the famous Locomotive No 41 at the train station ... but don't rush to catch it! Since 1960 it hasn't gone anywhere as the railway gauge was changed from narrow to 1.067mm gauge. A trainspotters' delight!

OUTJO ▼
Outjo revolves around cattle-ranching and one-night stay tourists en route to Etosha National Park, Khorixas or northern Kaokoland.

One of the town's most outstanding (literally) landmarks is the Water Tower, which has stood tall since 1901. The town museum is in Franke House, which dates back to 1899 and was one of Outjo's first homes. The museum shows off a wide range of minerals and gemstones, local history artifacts, and numerous animal skins, bones and horns ... and has a one-of-a-kind sheep-sheering device that operates off a bicycle chain! The nearby Ugab Terrace hills offer spectacular rock formations, including middle age castle shapes. Gamkarab Cave (50km away) boasts stalagmites and -tites of distinction.

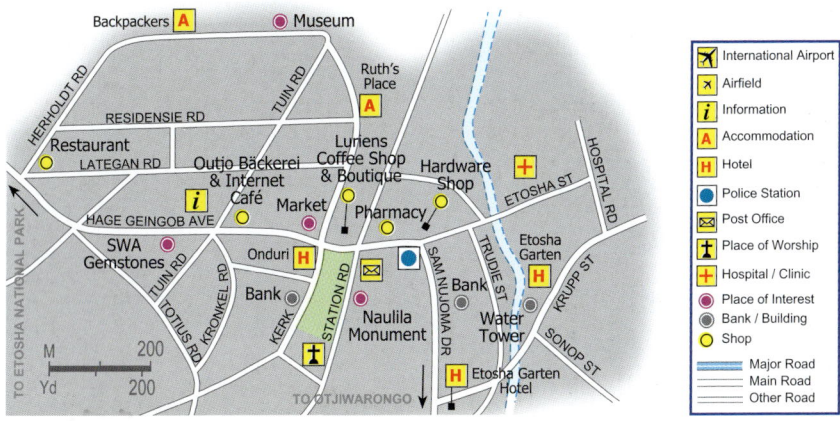

29

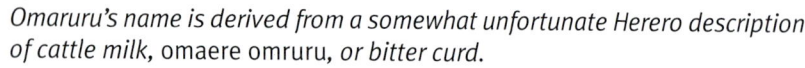

Omaruru's name is derived from a somewhat unfortunate Herero description of cattle milk, omaere omruru, *or bitter curd.*

Omaruru Omaruru Henties Bay He

OMARURU ▲
A dry river (most of the year) runs through the surprisingly green and pretty town of Omaruru. The major attraction in town is Franke Tower, which proudly commemorates the German captain who helped to repel the Hereros in 1904. More of the town's early history can be viewed in the museum at Mission House, Omaruru's oldest building. On the outskirts of town is the Kristall Kellerei (kellerei means 'cellars'), Namibia's first winery. Omaruru and its surroundings offer good birding opportunities, especially the possibility of ticking off some of the north-western endemics. Several game lodges in the area (which offer luxury accommodation) have been stocked with a wide variety of antelope, giraffe and rhino. The Erongo Massif near Omaruru is an excellent spot for rock climbers.

HENTIES BAY ▼
Hentie van der Merwe first started fishing here in 1929, and little did he know that a town would grow here and adopt his name. A sleepy hollow, Henties wakes up for the summer season to welcome the 10,000-plus visitors who flock to this fisherman's paradise, many with an eye on casting a line into the ocean or swinging their clubs at the 9-hole golf course that runs through a valley down towards the beach. The town has plenty of petrol stations to cater for the lack of supply further north.

Cape Fur Seals line the rocks and sand at Cape Cross, 60km north of Henties Bay.

Okahandja is renowned for offering some of the best fresh vegetables in Namibia, while Gobabis produces a third of the country's red meat.

obabis Gobabis Okahandja Okah

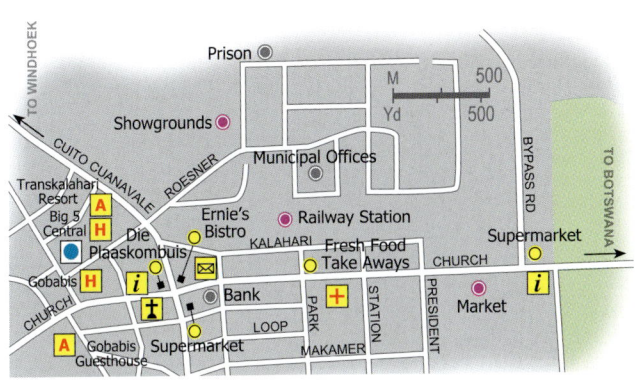

GOBABIS ▲
Gobabis has a special charm for passing tourists on this vital route through to Botswana. There are pretty old church buildings in town and a golf course. A statue of a bull at the town's western entrance bears testament to the importance of cattle to the Omaheke region, which has the second-highest number of cattle in all of Namibia's 13 regions.

🟨 Top Tip
The old experimental tobacco station in Okhandja is a photogenic building. It was started up in 1906 and hoped to capitalize on planting tobacco and rolling out cigars. Operations have long since ceased and the building is now empty and overgrown.

🟨 Top Trip
The farms around Gobabis offer game drives, but keep your eye out for the splendid sight of the local Herero women dressed in their traditional costumes.

Herero woman.

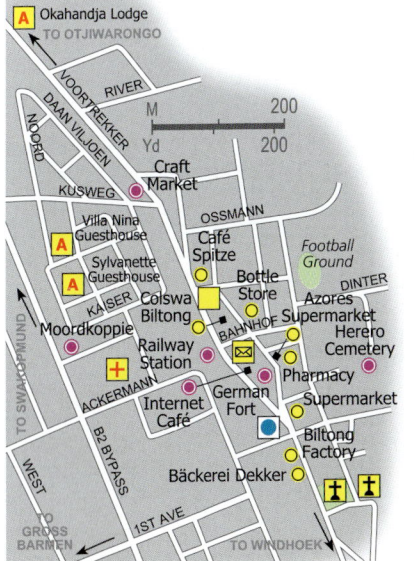

◀ OKAHANDJA
Okahandja might be small, but it boasts some of Namibia's finest open-air markets specializing in souvenirs such as wood-carvings (notably enormous hippos, huge giraffe and up to 2m tall human busts) as well as art from all around Namibia, Zimbabwe and even central Africa. The administrative 'capital' of the Herero, Okahandja hosts a large and colourful annual festival in August to honour the Herero forefathers. Okahandja is set in excellent farming country. There are numerous historic sights in and around town, including Moordkoppie (Murder Hill, the scene of the 1850 Herero massacre) and many graves of influential local leaders from the last 100 years (including that of the Oorlam leader Jan Jonker Afrikaner).

Rehoboth's hot springs were called Anhes (smoke) by the Swartbooi Namas because of the steam that rises from the hot water.

Mariental Mariental Rehoboth

REHOBOTH ▶
You have to see the Rehoboth museum (built in 1903, and found behind the post office) ... partly because there are few other attractions in town. Aside from a fascinating collection and display of bank notes and various items of local history, flora and fauna, you'll find a good history of the proud Baster people for whom Rehoboth is now their cultural home.

MARIENTAL ▼
Forget about peace and tranquility here: Mariental suffers from an unhappy climate. The heat is atrocious in summer, the cold is biting in winter, and the changes in season bring strong winds that blow dust everywhere. Local industry focusses on cultivating animal fodder, fruit and vegetables, as well as ostrich meat and karakul pelts, aided by its proximity to the Hardap Dam (Namibia's largest reservoir). Hardap itself is enjoyed by anglers, hikers, birders and boating enthusiasts. The town owes its name to Herman Brandt, the first colonial settler in the area, who made his wife happy by naming it Marie's Valley (hence Mariental).

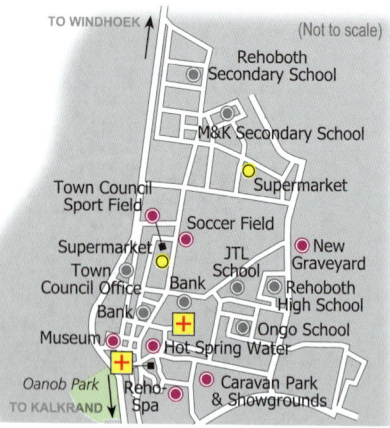

Top Tip: Rehoboth's spa offers a pleasant hot spring enjoyed by the Nama for centuries, though now somewhat the worse for wear. Oanob Lake Resort is becoming increasingly popular for watersports, hiking and birdwatching.

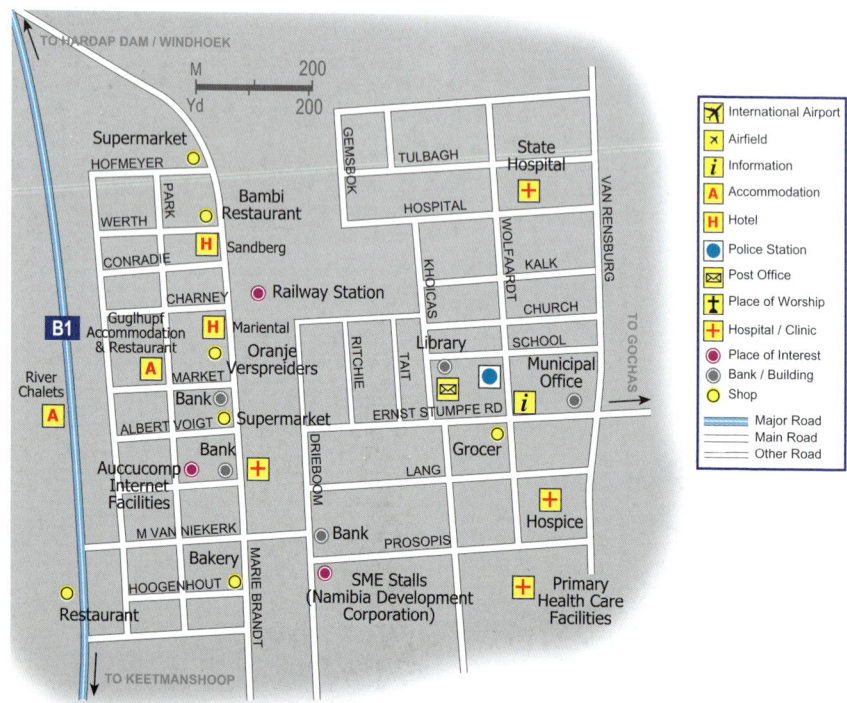

32

The hub of the Karakul wool industry, Keetmanshoop is the 'capital of the south' and its road junction links Lüderitz, South Africa and Windhoek.

Keetmanshoop Keetmanshoop Keet

Keetmanshoop (shortened to 'Keet' by the locals) is a sunny town with attractive German colonial architecture, pretty gardens and a rustic museum. 'Keet' is situated almost 500km south of Windhoek and roughly 1,000m above sea level. The original church was built in 1866 but, alas, 24 years later a freak flood washed the entire building away! Its replacement (the current town museum) was put up five years later ... this time on somewhat higher ground!

Keetmanshoop museum.

33

Key Touring Maps

Key Touring Maps Key Touring M

Namibia represents an uneasy compromise between man and nature to carve out their territory of choice. Jagged and – in places – treacherous natural borders were created by centuries of persistent erosion by the mighty Atlantic Ocean, while the top and bottom of this vast land have been chipped away by great rivers with memories deeper than humankind: the Orange, Cunene, Kavango, Zambezi and Chobe. Where nature failed to penetrate the remaining borders, man stepped in to rule straight lines of territorial control. This strange shape for such a stark yet hauntingly beautiful land befits a country that has seen much pain and suffering. It's as though someone had tried to tame the land, but nature reminds travellers and settlers that it can't be harnessed, can't be approached lightly or without caution. It allows man to take dangerous liberties as his pride and courage urge him to conquer the elements.
Yet always Namibia will win.
This is a land which is a great ally, but an even greater enemy.

Etosha ('great white place' in Herero, due to the bright sun) is one of the finest game reserves to be found in Southern Africa.

Etosha Etosha Etosha Etosha Eto

Etosha is a vital game reserve for the entire Southern Africa region and is home to 114 species of mammal, 340 bird species, 110 different reptiles, 16 species of amphibians and yet just one fish species. All this is found in the 22,000km² that makes up the park named after the massive pan that covers a vast 5,000km², stretching roughly 120km from east to west and some 70km across at its widest point. The pan seldom boasts much water (if any) as it is fed by the rains rather than reliable rivers, and even when the rains fall hard few areas fill up or flood due to the incredibly high rate of evaporation. The rainy season signals the arrival of summer migrants in the form of

Oryx (or gemsbok) tend to congregate around Etosha's waterholes.

Etosha is best explored in your own car without a guide. The roads are good and the open landscape allows for excellent wildlife spotting.

Etosha Etosha Etosha Etosha Etos

mammals and birds. In good years the pan will be alive with thousands of flamingoes. The western reaches of Etosha feature some unique areas, including the fascinating Moringa Forest or Haunted Forest (dubbed *Sprokieswoud* in Afrikaans) with its weirdly contorted moringa trees – possibly shaped by browsing herds of elephant and giraffe. Etosha has three main rest camps (Namutoni, Halali and Okaukuejo) with perimeter fencing and superb floodlit waterholes which are open 24 hours a day. The world's largest game reserve until the 1960s, when its surface area was reduced by nearly 80%, Etosha remains one of the largest and most important parks in Africa.

A lioness defending her territory. She also has to do the bulk of the hunting to feed the pride.

37

The name Naukluft means 'narrow ravine'. This dramatic landscape is much loved by hikers, four-wheel drive enthusiasts and photographers alike.

Sossusvlei Namib-Naukluft Sossu

Larger than Switzerland, the 50,000km²-plus of fantastically scenic desert landscape occupied by the Namib-Naukluft Park ranks it with the biggest in all of Africa. It represents a vital conservation effort to retain the pristine nature of the Namib desert, which vies with the Atacama Desert in South America for the title of oldest on earth. You'll need plenty of time to enjoy all that the park has to offer, so keep your itinerary flexible. The Namib has an amazing array of wildlife, with many plants found in the mountainous region, an area enjoyed by the rare Hartmann's mountain zebra as well as leopards and other shy animals who appreciate the vegetation and sanctuary offered by the many caves, gorges and rocky terrain. There are also numerous small nocturnal delights (insects and reptiles) to be found throughout the area, while birdwatchers will delight in the bustling air traffic around the deep kloof which has water throughout the year. Horse-riding and hiking are popular ways to traverse much of this region, with hikes ranging from a few hours up to the more advanced eight-day, 120km Naukluft Hiking Trail.

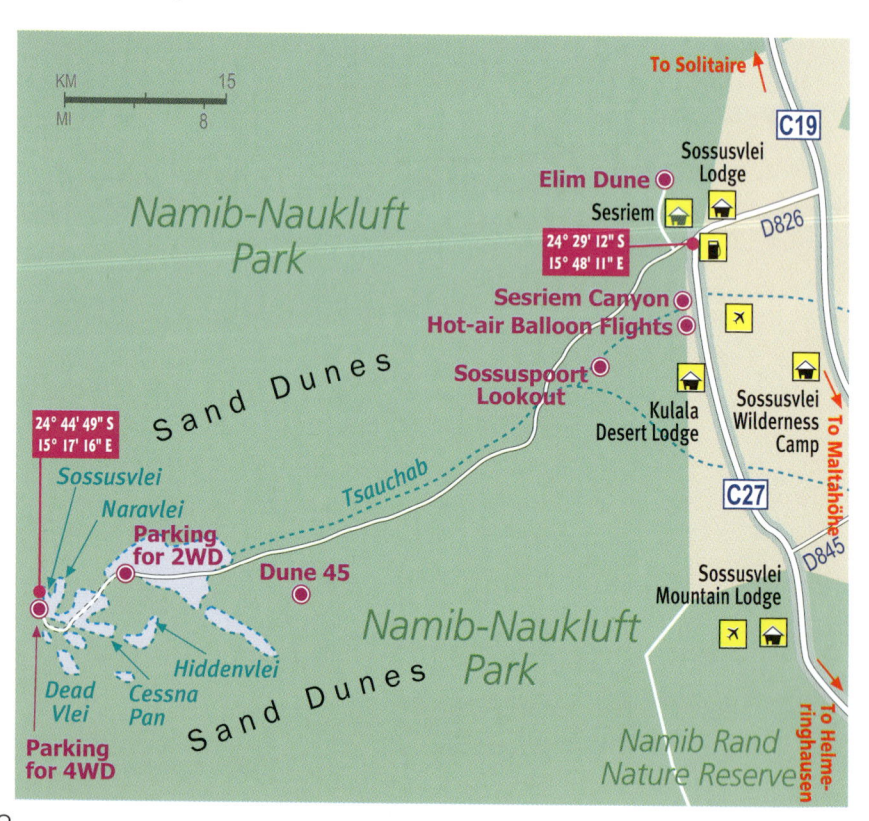

Sossusvlei's Dead Pan is surrounded by dunes and filled with long-dead trees.

Sesriem Canyon derives its name from ses riem *(six thongs), the number of rope lengths needed to draw water from the 30m deep gorge.*

Namib-Naukluft Sossusvlei Nam

Sossusvlei, with its stark yet striking beauty, is one of the natural world's great photo opportunities. The occasional rain quickly sinks into the thirsty ground – it sustains hardy camel thorn acacias and the indestructible *!nara*, a melon-bearing plant that offers vital nourishment to a variety of animals in this unforgiving territory. The skeletal remains of ancient trees in Dead Vlei (some of which lived centuries ago) are all that remains of easier times, when rain was more plentiful and sustained a variety of flora. Lovers of sand and dunes will be in their element at Sossusvlei as the vlei (pan) is surrounded by one of the world's tallest sand dunes. These can rise 300m and are best viewed as the early morning sun breaks the horizon, highlighting the redness of the sand. The sand at Sesriem (which acts as the gateway to Sossusvlei) is ocean sand blown inland. A number of camps, lodges and campsites allow visitors quick access (by foot, 4WD or shuttle) to this dramatic landscape with its great walking opportunities and fascinating geological formations.

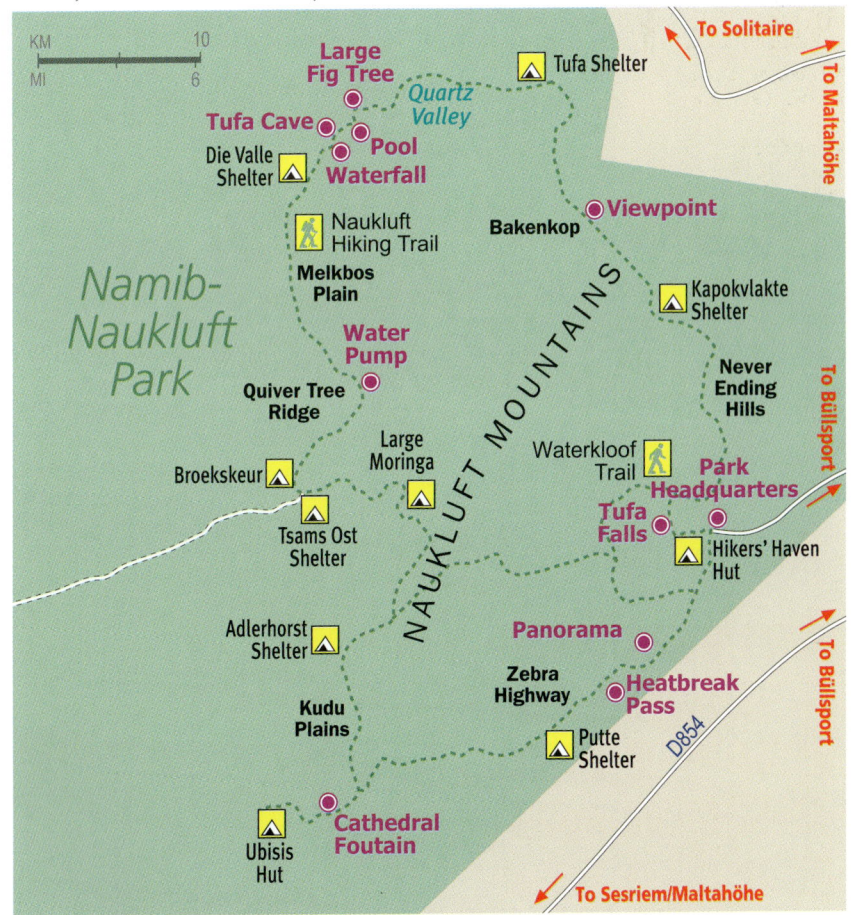

Sossusvlei's glowing red dunes.

39

Kaokoland is rugged and remote. Entrusting your travel arrangements to someone who does not know it intimately is simply asking for trouble.

Kaokoland Kaokoland Kaokoland

The Kaokoland presents one of Namibia's greatest challenges: a vast stretch of land that is alluring yet utterly inhospitable to all but the local Himbas and extremely well-prepared travellers. Located in north-west Namibia, Kaokoland is an extremely barren mountain desert region, offering little in the way of water or vegetation, yet despite its desolation it displays a unique beauty. Its floral delights are spectacular, bottle trees rising from rocky *koppies* (hills) boldly defying the elements. Look closely and tread carefully and you will discover a wide range of succulents underfoot. Animals are scarce, the legacy of unscrupulous hunting, poaching and the unfortunate large-scale slaughter of wildlife for food during the desperate struggle for independence. If you're in luck you'll come across cheetah, leopard and lion, or some of the small herds of springbok and gemsbok, in addition to zebra and giraffe. The area is perhaps more famed for the presence of black rhino (Kaokoland is the black rhino's last free-roaming area on earth) and the desert elephant. These hardy elephants have extra-long legs to help them trudge the barren land, up to 70km a day, looking for nourishment. They can survive

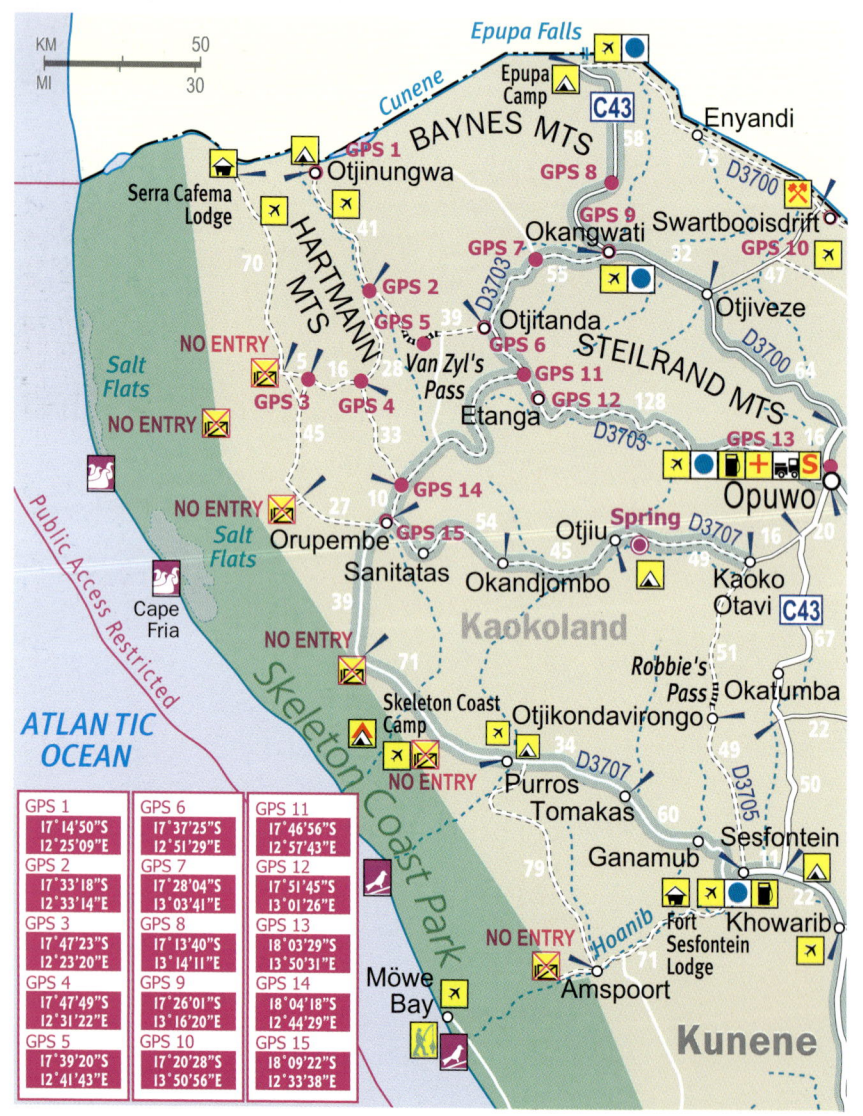

GPS 1	GPS 6	GPS 11
17°14'50"S	17°37'25"S	17°46'56"S
12°25'09"E	12°51'29"E	12°57'43"E
GPS 2	GPS 7	GPS 12
17°33'18"S	17°28'04"S	17°51'45"S
12°33'14"E	13°03'41"E	13°01'26"E
GPS 3	GPS 8	GPS 13
17°47'23"S	17°13'40"S	18°03'29"S
12°23'20"E	13°14'11"E	13°50'31"E
GPS 4	GPS 9	GPS 14
17°47'49"S	17°26'01"S	18°04'18"S
12°31'22"E	13°16'20"E	12°44'29"E
GPS 5	GPS 10	GPS 15
17°39'20"S	17°20'28"S	18°09'22"S
12°41'43"E	13°50'56"E	12°33'38"E

The Kaokoland's terrain might be tough and unforgiving, but it remains fragile: some tyre tracks made decades earlier remain to this day.

Kaokoland Kaokoland Kaokoland Kaok

for up to five days without water. The area is dangerous for travellers, as the searing heat and barren environment offer little sustenance for those trapped without transport, roads often get washed away in the rain, while dry riverbeds have quicksand spots that have been known to swallow vehicles. Travellers should not consider tackling this harsh territory without at least one other vehicle in tow, an experienced navigator and meticulous planning and preparation. Aside from personal safety, be extremely sensitive to the environment when driving overland. There are numerous rough paths, but make sure that you always stick to existing tracks as this will limit the damage to vegetation and animals. Try to avoid unnecessary driving or joy-riding over sandy areas in particular. Flanked by baobabs on either side, the Cunene River to the north offers a wide range of water-based diversions to cater for all tastes and levels of courage and skill.

Top Tip

The Cunene River boasts numerous water-sport opportunities to cater for mild to wild interests. The surrounding vegetation (lush by Kaokoland standards!) acts like a magnet for wildlife and tourists alike.

Kaokoland's varying landscapes.

41

Loch Ness has nothing on the Fish River Canyon: local legend claims that the mighty meanders in the canyon were caused by a massive snake!

Fish River Canyon

One of Africa's great natural wonders (and one of the world's largest canyons, behind America's Grand Canyon), the Fish River Canyon provides an awesome spectacle as well as an abundance of adventure activities. The canyon itself is massive, 500m deep and over 25km wide in some places, and stretching a distance of around 160km. Part of the Ai-Ais conservation area, the canyon lies near Namibia's southern border, offering easy access from South Africa. The Ai-Ais rest camp, on the banks of the Fish River, accommodates most of the canyon's visitors. It is located near the hot springs in the canyon (Ai-Ais means very hot in the Nama tongue) and is surrounded by dramatic lunar-like landscape.

It is possible to visit the canyon without spending a night in Ai-Ais (if your budget or schedule is tight), as day-trips can be made from Keetmanshoop and other nearby bases. This will, however, limit the time available to explore the canyon and indulge in all the acitivities offered by lodges and rest camps in the area: horse-riding, day hikes (with or without a guide), overnight hikes and camping (such as at Hobas, which is close to the canyon's main viewpoint), driving trips, animal- and bird-watching, or simple walks to the viewing spots to enjoy the unforgettable vistas. The ultimate experience is a flight over the canyon with views that go on forever – a memory that will last a lifetime. The canyon contains deposits of sandstone, shale and lava millions of years old. The geology around the Canyon, and along its seemingly endless course, is fascinating, with scores of amazing rock formations, intrusive granites and dolerite dykes.

Forming the natural border between South Africa and Namibia, the Orange (or Gariep) River offers a variety of water adventures, from gently drifting down the river from one riverside camp to the next, to adrenaline-pumping white-water bashes over rocks and rapids that can challenge (and terrify) even the most experienced rivermen. River trips generally range from four to six days and can be combined with a five-day horseback trail if you have any energy and nerve left.

Right: *The tiny klipspringer (half a metre at the shoulder) can elude any predator ... so long as the chase is over rocky terrain.*
Below: *A view from the bottom of the canyon.*

The popular Ai-Ais hot springs oasis on the banks of the Fish River has experienced temperatures of 47 °C.

Fish River Canyon Fish River Canyon

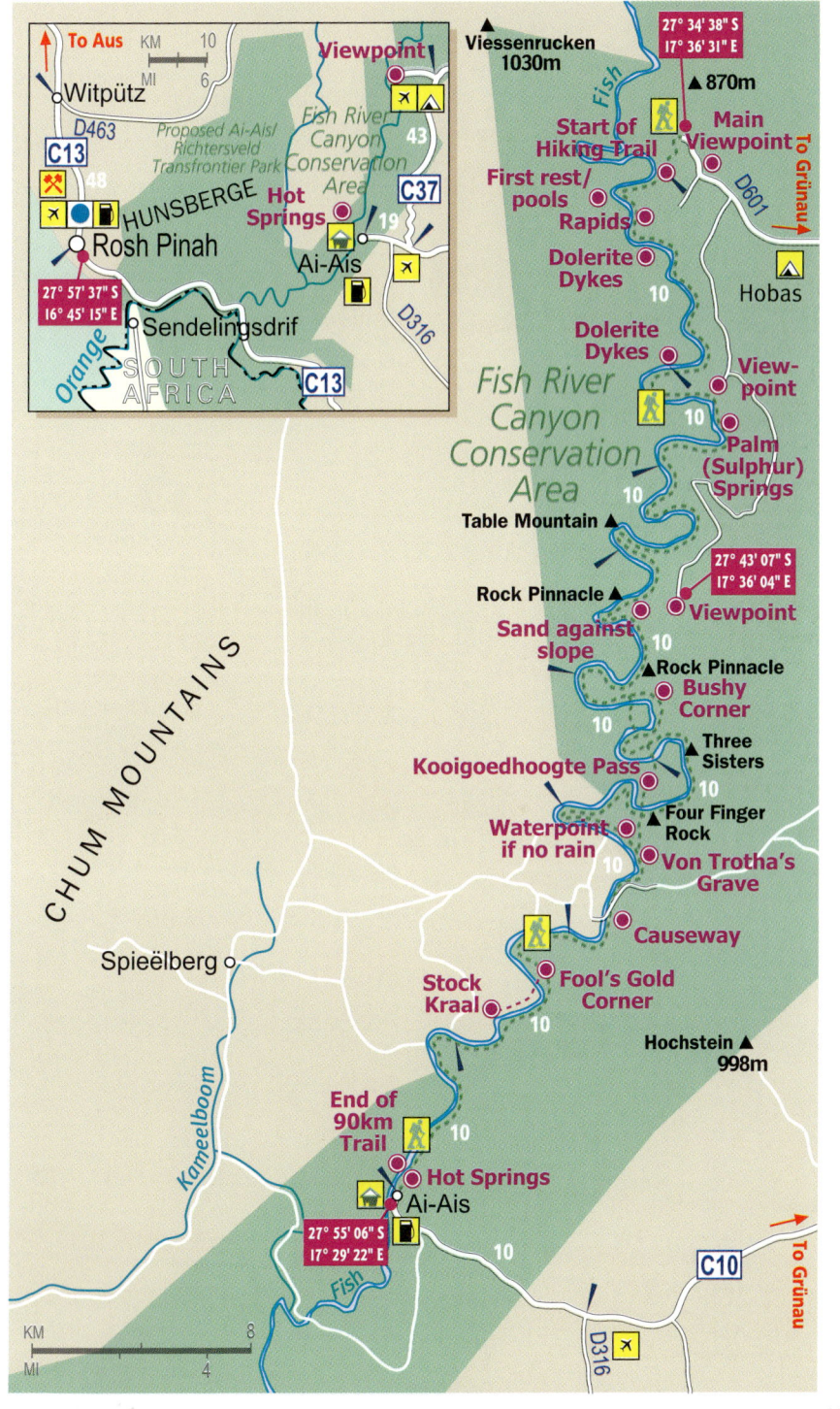

Inset map
To Aus · Witpütz · D463 · C13 · HUNSBERGE · Rosh Pinah · Proposed Ai-Ais/Richtersveld Transfrontier Park · Fish River Canyon Conservation Area · Hot Springs · Ai-Ais · C37 · D316 · Sendelingsdrif · Orange · SOUTH AFRICA · C13 · 27° 57' 37" S 16° 45' 15" E

Main map labels
- Viewpoint
- Viessenrucken 1030m
- 27° 34' 38" S 17° 36' 31" E
- 870m
- Start of Hiking Trail
- Main Viewpoint
- To Grünau
- D601
- First rest/pools
- Rapids
- Dolerite Dykes
- Hobas
- Dolerite Dykes
- Viewpoint
- Fish River Canyon Conservation Area
- Palm (Sulphur) Springs
- Table Mountain
- Rock Pinnacle
- 27° 43' 07" S 17° 36' 04" E
- Viewpoint
- Sand against slope
- Rock Pinnacle
- Bushy Corner
- Three Sisters
- Kooigoedhoogte Pass
- Four Finger Rock
- Waterpoint if no rain
- Von Trotha's Grave
- Causeway
- CHUM MOUNTAINS
- Spieëlberg
- Stock Kraal
- Fool's Gold Corner
- Hochstein 998m
- Kameelboom
- End of 90km Trail
- Hot Springs
- Ai-Ais
- 27° 55' 06" S 17° 29' 22" E
- C10
- To Grünau
- D316
- Fish

43

!Nara melons, endemic to the Namib desert, are a valuable food source for desert scavengers as well as a traditional food of the Topnaar Namas.

Namib-Naukluft Park & West Coa

Previously known as the Namib Desert Park, the Namib section of the Namib-Naukluft Park (Africa's third-largest nature reserve, Park) offers plenty of worthwhile attractions, including the majestic cliffs and ravines of the Kuiseb Canyon, with plenty of overnight and four-wheel drive opportunities. Widely regarded as the oldest desert on earth, it is believed that the Namib Desert has 'enjoyed' its arid to semi-arid conditions for as long as 80 million years. The West Coast offers fantastic hiking and driving trips (especially along the Skeleton Coast), as well as excellent fishing. A treacherous coastline over the centuries, many ships have run aground here. It's harshness is typified in the landmark Bogenfels Arch which is, unfortunately, no longer accessible to the public.

The dramatic Bogenfels Arch, a 50m-high rock arch south of Lüderitz on the West Coast.

The wetlands at Sandwich Harbour offer a haven for birds, and the unspoilt coastline and spectacular scenery make it a popular tourist stop.

amib-Naukluft Park & West Coast

Four-wheel drive trips along the Skeleton Coast offer a unique driving experience, yet it demands caution and a large degree of consideration for the environment.

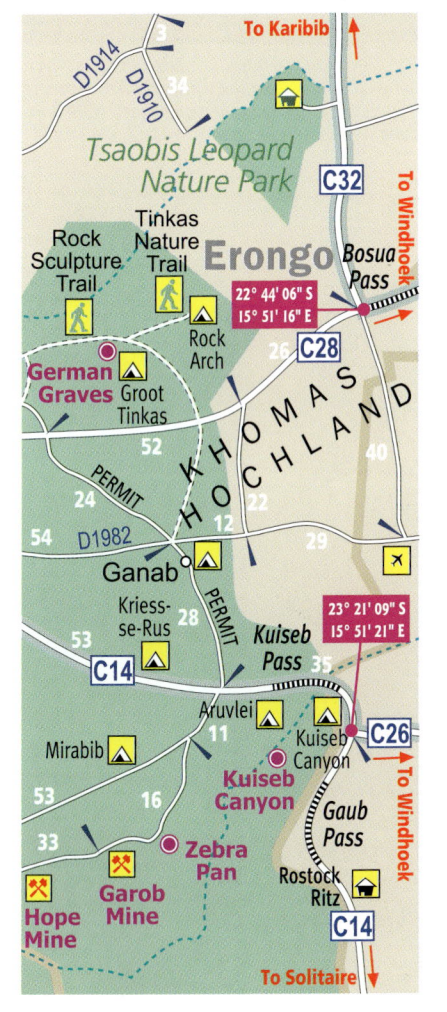

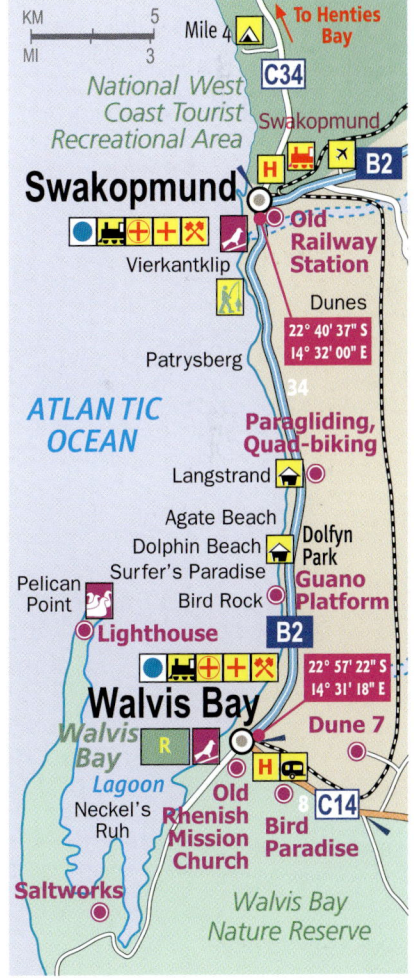

45

> Driving in two-vehicle (at least) convoys in Mamili National Park is strongly advised ... regardless of your perceived survival skills.

Mamili

The 32,000ha Mamili National Park was opened at the same time as Mudumu (1990), and they act as the eastern Caprivi's only protected areas. The Linyandi Swamp are a major drawcard when the Kwando River is running full (often flooding around June), which provides lazy mokoro (dugout) trips to explore the forested islands, wetlands and reeded channels. Naturally, there is abundant birdlife (more than 430 species) in addition to other wildlife (from elephant to lion, giraffe and hippo, along with numerous buck), despite the past ravages of poachers' weapons. Mokoro and 4WD are the only way to get around Mamili. This is not the place to take personal risks, as help can be a long time coming. There are rangers on patrol throughout the park, but they might not cross your path in time if you've found your way into a spot of difficulty. Gameviewing is best before the rainy season, which can start as early as October. The best birding opportunities are between December and March when the migrants move in, but then the 'black cotton' clay (road) tracks could become totally inaccessible.

The African jacana has unusually long toes which are well adapted for the wetland environments it frequents: the long toes allow it to walk and even run on floating plants without sinking.

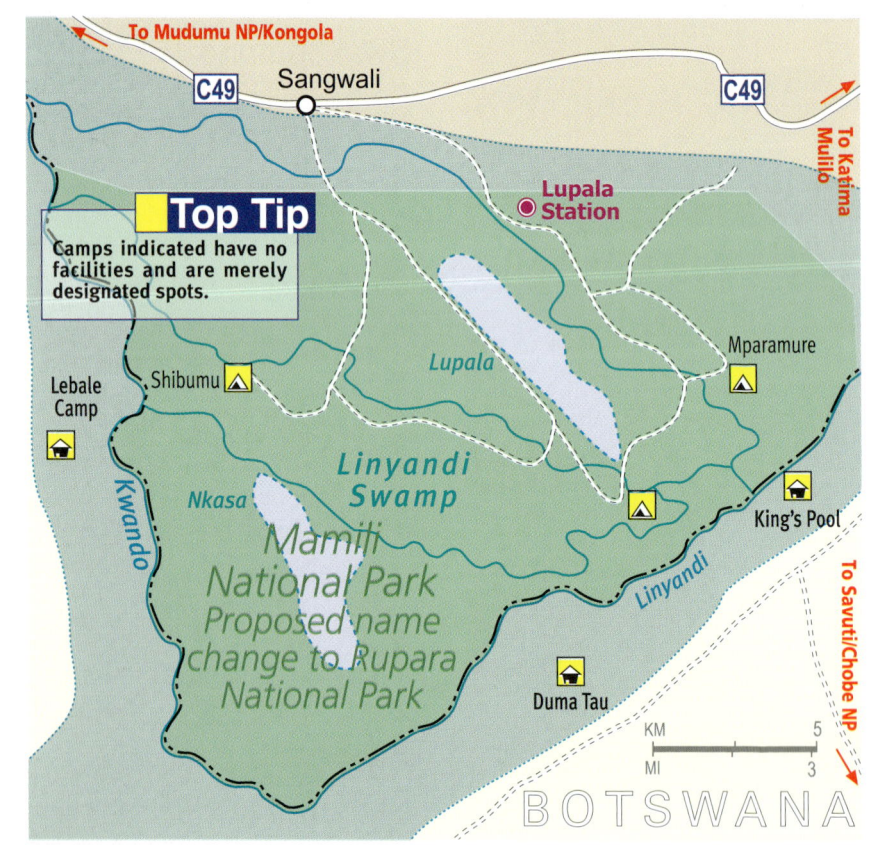

Top Tip
Camps indicated have no facilities and are merely designated spots.

46

> Mudumu was renowned as Namibia's greatest wildlife habitat before the ravages of poaching took their toll, but the park remains alive with fauna.

Mudumu Mudumu Mudumu Mudu

Spread across 100,000ha, Mudumu is hugged to the west by the Kwando River, which is alive with crocodile, hippo and numerous water-loving buck (sitatunga, red lechwe and reedbuck). Covered in mopane woodlands, the reserve is well-populated with elephant, giraffe and zebra, in addition to impala, kudu, red lechwe and the somewhat uncommon roan antelope species. These animals enjoy the shelter and foliage offered by the abundant mopane. Bird-watchers will fall in love with Mudumu, especially if they get to spot the African Fish Eagle, the Narina trogon, Pel's fishing owl, or any of the many species found nowhere else in Namibia. It's best to explore Mudumu by 4WD, but Lianshulu Lodge and Lianshulu Bush Lodge offer guided walks. For a cultural diversion, visit the Lizauli Traditional Village just outside Mudumu to learn about traditional Caprivi lifestyles (from food to farming methods, medicine to crafts and toolmaking). Lizauli is one of many local upliftment programmes and is worth supporting if you are environmentally or culturally sensitive.

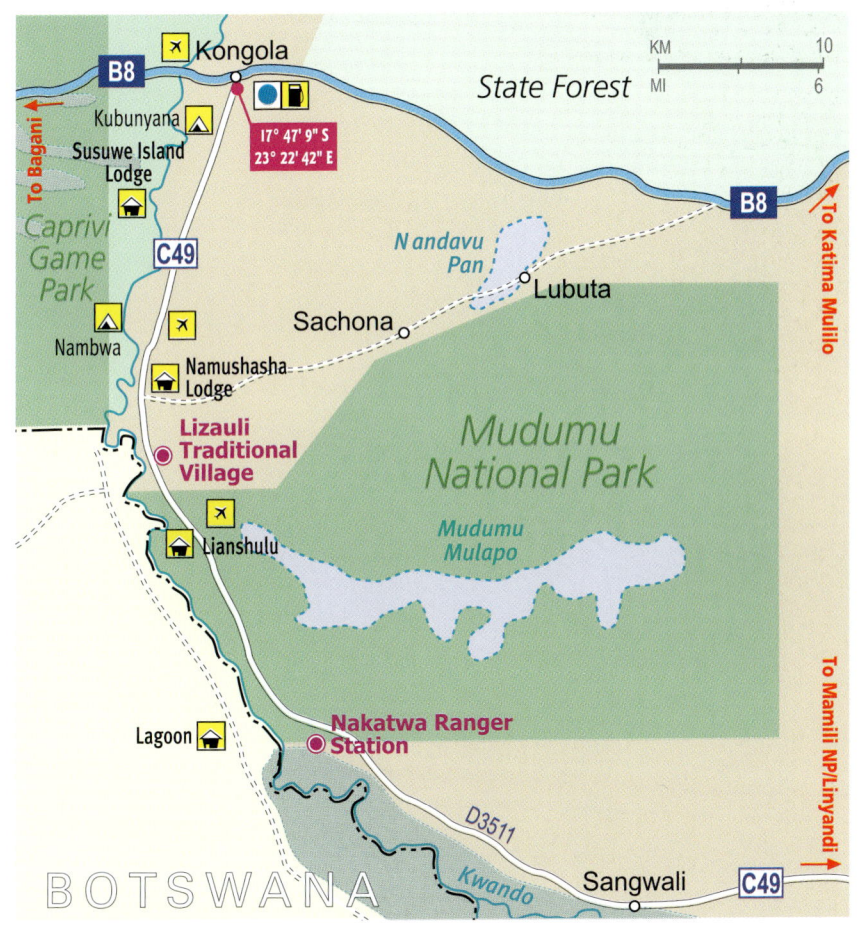

Burchell's zebra enjoy the mopane-rich environment of the Mudumu National Park.

47

> Khaudum is wild, four-wheel drive country. Its remoteness might add to its charm, but it demands travelling in a group with adequate supplies.

Khaudum Game Reserve

The lack of fencing around Khaudum (with the exception of the boundary with Botswana) allows animals to leave the park in search of fresh grazing and water during the rainy season, thus ensuring an abundance of wildlife to enjoy, particularly wild dogs and roan antelope. Game viewing is best in winter, as long as you have patience and discipline: these free-roaming animals don't take kindly to noise, particularly from humans and their vehicles! The artificial waterholes provide some of the best wildlife spotting. Heavier summer rain thickens the dry woodland savannah (located on settled parts of the Kalahari's sand dunes), which encourages an abundance of birdlife for 'twitchers' to enjoy.

Sunset in the Khaudum Game Reserve.

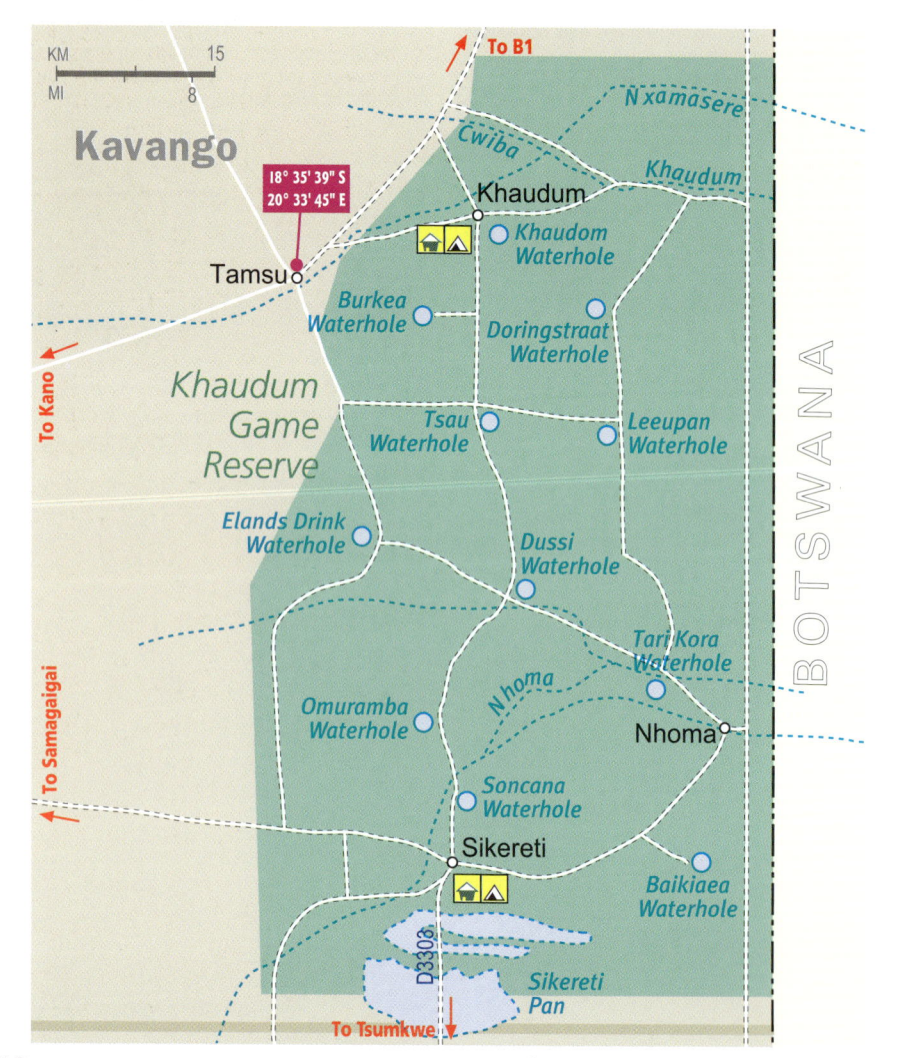

The Waterberg Plateau is centred totally on the animals and their needs. Tourists may not drive themselves around and must fit in with the animals.

Waterberg Plateau Park

The Waterberg Plateau dominates the surrounding landscape, its steep cliffs rise hundreds of metres above the surrounding plains, making the plateau a safe haven for wildlife. Many of Namibia's endangered species have been rehomed here to protect them from poachers and predators alike. This animal paradise towers a breathtaking 1,800m-plus above sea level and, aided by an amazing biodiversity which enables this small park to support a wide array of animals, it is a conservation success that actually supplies rare species of game and wildlife to many of Namibia's other parks. You can drive around the park on one of the limited, organized game drive ... but NOT on your own. The animals prefer it that way! Walking in the park provides incredible scenery and game viewing opportunities. The attractions include more than 200 species of birds (with black eagles and Cape vultures), as well as age-old dinosaur tracks and numerous examples of San rock art.

A natural still life in the Waterberg.

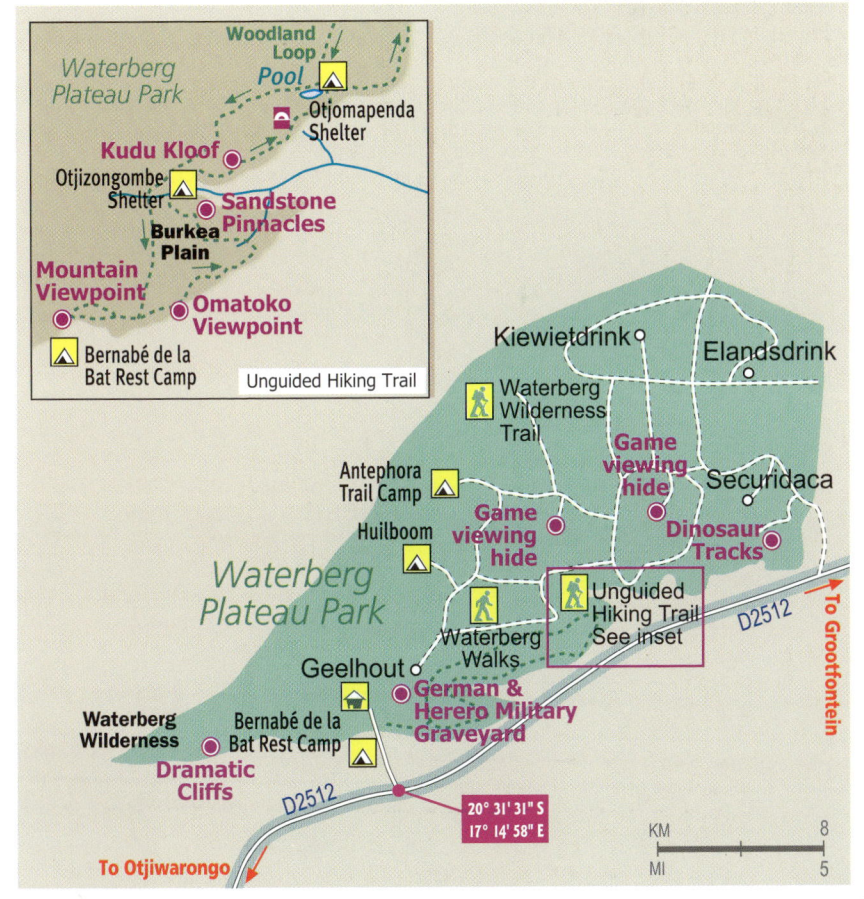

49

Hardap Dam's capacity amounts to 323 million cubic meters of water held by a 39m-high, 865m-long dam wall, and offering a surface area of 25km².

Hardap Hardap Lüderitz Peninsula

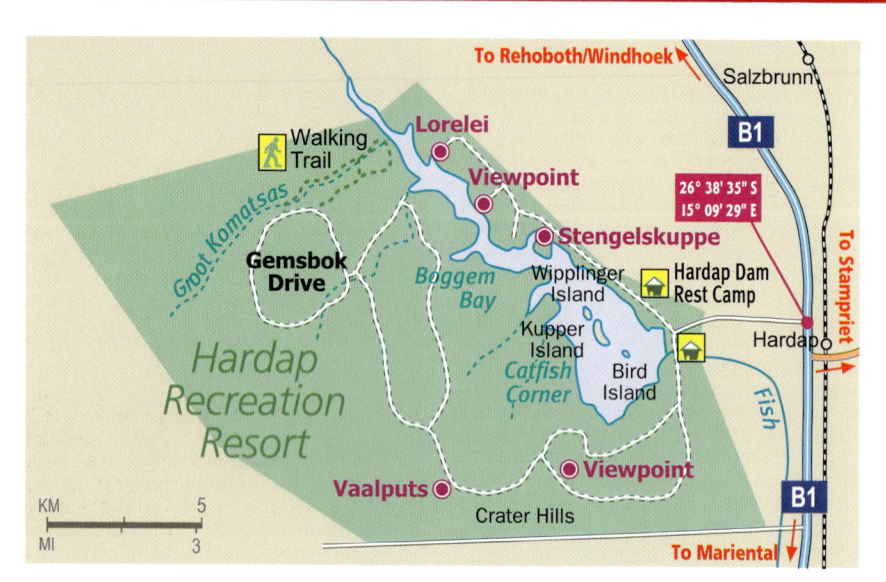

LÜDERITZ PENINSULA
A trip around the peninsula (in calm weather) will offer up some fabulous views and swimming possibilities at one of the many bays along the coast (Dias Point and Griffith Bay offer stunning views), while the rusted remnants of Sturmvogel Bucht's 'deceased' Norwegian Whaling Station is worth a look.

HARDAP GAME RESERVE
Hardap covers 23,420ha and offers driving trails as well as excellent predator-free walking trails, especially around Crater Hills (named for the rough terrain it encloses). The birdlife is superb thanks to the large dam, with over 250 species spotted here, including the majestic African Fish Eagle.

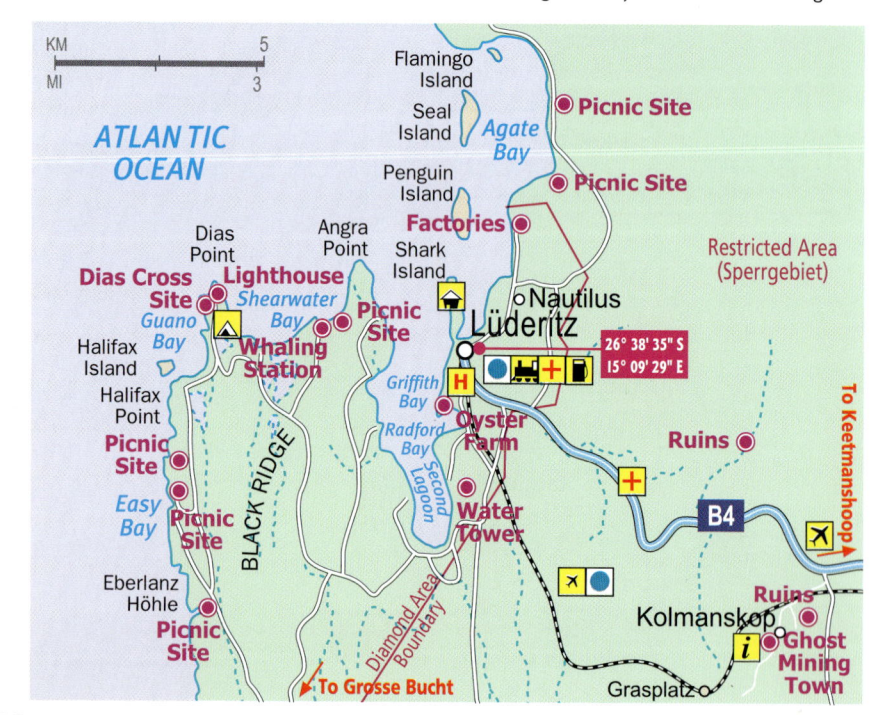

Most of Kolmanskop's buildings remain as they were 40 years ago when its inhabitants left, leaving the desert sand to invade.

olmanskop Kolmanskop Kolmansk

The ghostly interior of a Kolmanskop house.

The desert ghost-town of Kolmanskop is accessible for visitors, lying just 10km from Lüderitz. The diamond boom saw this town spring up in 1908 and become the centre of the region's diamond industry. During its boom years the streets and businesses bustled with determined prospectors, stars in their eyes, readily diving into the desert's sands in search of their fortunes. Its attraction now is as a tourist stop to explore the sand-ravaged ghost town, 'dead' for over 40 years ... so you won't be able to enjoy the town's former facilities of an ice factory, casino and excellent theatre, although the skittle alley has been restored to working order.

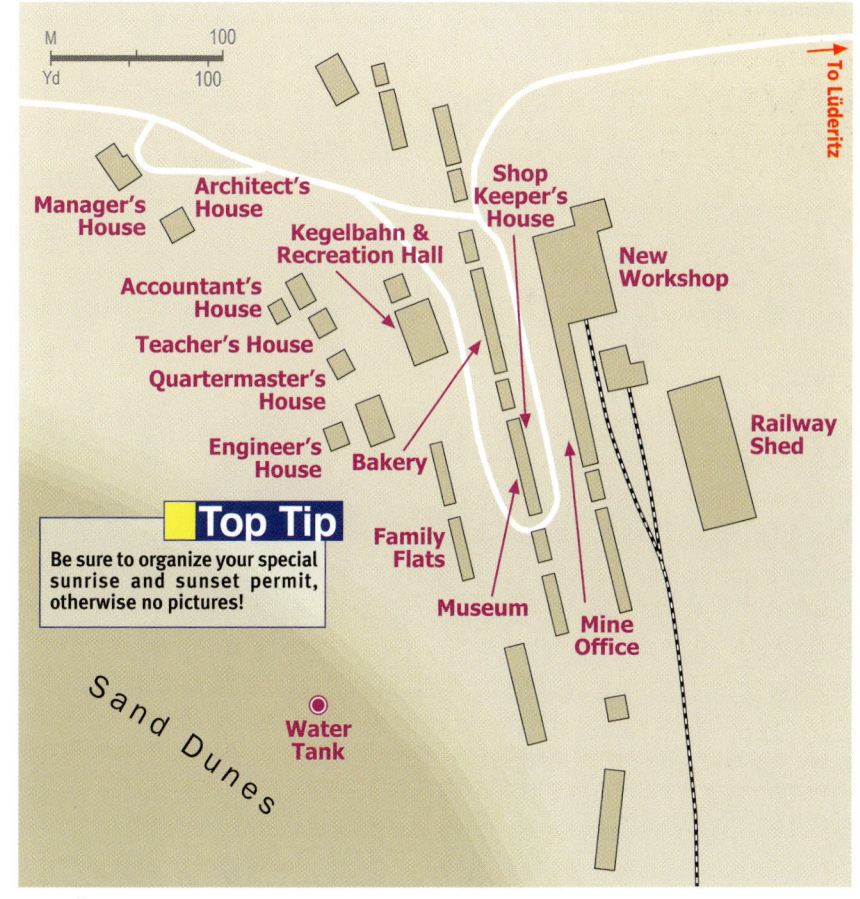

Top Tip
Be sure to organize your special sunrise and sunset permit, otherwise no pictures!

51

Touring/Driving Maps Touring/Driv

Maps Touring/Driving Maps Tour

Namibia's long, straight roads demand from travellers time, patience and endurance as they draw you vast distances between the country's many cultural attractions, which range from colonial outposts and strongholds through to the many traditional villages that dot the landscape. The road will also lead you through and into Namibia's many varied wilderness areas, game reserves and national parks, offering vast openness, scores of animals roaming free and great deserts untrappable by man.

A standard vehicle will take you across Namibia's 5,200km of tarred roads, but a four-wheel drive is essential to explore the true depths of Namibia's 35,000km of gravel roads and other unchartered territory. However, even these hardy vehicles can fall prey to the dunes, rocky terrain and sporadic quicksand that await you once you veer off the beaten track. Trying to cut corners or pushing too hard to reach your destination on schedule is your best way to get into the sort of trouble that could dig a hole in your pocket, or worse!

Map

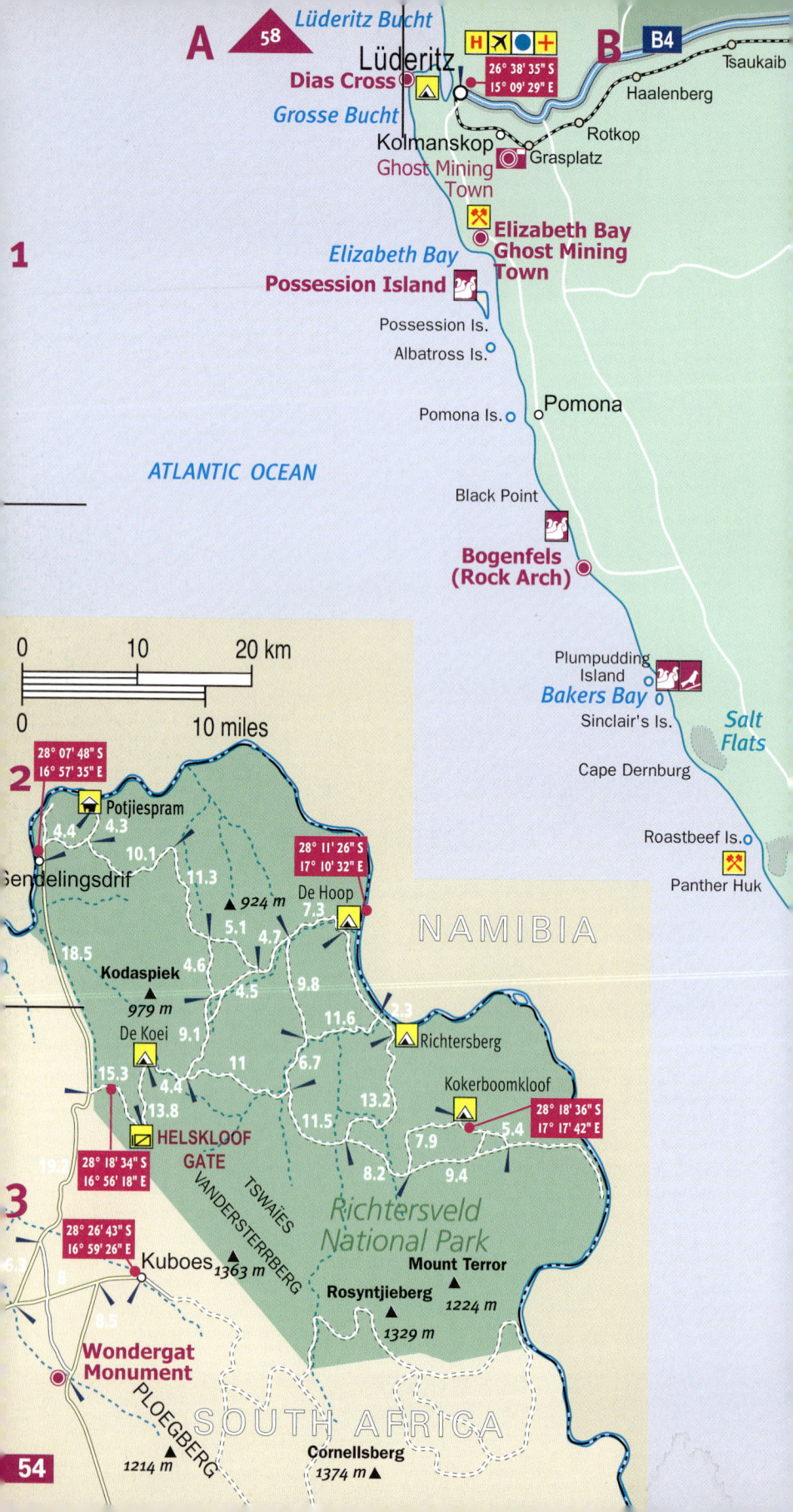

A — 58

Lüderitz Bucht
Lüderitz
Dias Cross
26° 38' 35" S
15° 09' 29" E
Grosse Bucht
Kolmanskop
Ghost Mining Town

B — B4
Tsaukaib
Haalenberg
Rotkop
Grasplatz

Elizabeth Bay
Possession Island
Elizabeth Bay Ghost Mining Town
Possession Is.
Albatross Is.
Pomona Is.
Pomona

1

ATLANTIC OCEAN

Black Point
Bogenfels (Rock Arch)

Plumpudding Island
Bakers Bay
Sinclair's Is.
Cape Dernburg
Salt Flats
Roastbeef Is.
Panther Huk

0 — 10 — 20 km
0 — 10 miles

2
28° 07' 48" S
16° 57' 35" E
Potjiespram
4.4 4.3
10.1
11.3
▲ 924 m
28° 11' 26" S
17° 10' 32" E
De Hoop
5.1 4.7
7.3
Sendelingsdrif
18.5
Kodaspiek
4.6
▲ 979 m
4.5
9.8
NAMIBIA
De Koei
9.1
11.6
2.3
Richtersberg
11
6.7
Kokerboomkloof
15.3
4.4
13.2
28° 18' 36" S
17° 17' 42" E
13.8
HELSKLOOF GATE
11.5
7.9 5.4
28° 18' 34" S
16° 56' 18" E
8.2 9.4
19.2
TSWAÏES
VANDERSTERRBERG
Richtersveld National Park

3
28° 26' 43" S
16° 59' 26" E
Kuboes
▲ 1363 m
Mount Terror
Rosyntjieberg ▲
▲ 1224 m
▲ 1329 m
8.5
Wondergat Monument
PLOEGBERG
SOUTH AFRICA
▲ 1214 m
Cornellsberg
▲ 1374 m

54

Map: Southern Namibia / Northern South Africa

Places and Features

- Garub
- Ausweiche
- Aus
- Klein-Aus Vista
- Ausnek
- Asbospan
- Guibes
- Goageb
- Aukam
- Huns
- Witpütz
- Rosh Pinah
- Ferry Crossing
- Sendelingsdrif
- Kuboes
- Oranjemund
- Alexander Bay
- Wreck Point
- Eksteenfontein
- Lekkersing

Regions

- **HUIB-HOCH PLATEAU** (1700m)
- **KLINGHARD MTS**
- **HUNSBERGE**
- **Ai-Ais / Richtersveld Transfrontier Park**
- **Richtersveld National Park** (SEE ENLARGED MAP ON PAGE 54)
- **Restricted Area (Former Sperrgebiet)**
- **NAMIBIA**
- **SOUTH AFRICA**
- Orange (Gariep) river
- Holgat
- Konkiep

Roads

- C13, B4, C14, D435, D446, D727, D463, D459

Coordinates

- Aus: 26° 39' 47" S, 16° 15' 49" E
- Goageb: 26° 45' 19" S, 17° 13' 40" E
- Rosh Pinah: 27° 57' 37" S, 16° 45' 15" E
- Oranjemund: 28° 33' 12" S, 16° 25' 57" E

Grid references

C, D, 55, 56, 59

NO ENTRY

Oranjemund R

A
B
1
2
3
Old Fort
26° 47' 53" S 17° 48' 45" E
60
Gobas
Coenbult
Goageb
B4
Jurgen
Seeheim
Sandverhaar
Feldschuhhorn
Naute
Naute Recreation Area
Löwen
D578
Narubis
M26
Gawagab
Inachab
D459
D432
D463
D545
D608
D607
Karas
2202m
1559m
C12
Huns
55
Holoog
Cañon Roadhouse
C37
Fish River Canyon
Viewpoint
Gorges
Klein-Karas
B1
GROOT
HUNSBERGE
Fish River Canyon Conservation Area
Cañon Lodge
Signalberg
D298
27° 43' 26" S 18° 22' 40" E
D270
D203
Grünau
B3
Nanzes
Konkiep
Hot Springs
Fish River Canyon Hiking Trail
Ai-Ais
C10
(D601)
Kanus
28° 01' 10" S 18° 45' 15" E
Satco
27° 56' 30" S 18° 10' 39" E
Karasburg
M22
(D207)
D316
D208
C2
ichtersveld National Park
D210
D213
Warmbad Hot Springs
C13
Orange (Gariep)
Aussenkehr
NAMIBIA
Hom
Haib
28° 45' 03" S 17° 37' 15" E
Noordoewer
Vioolsdrif
NOORDOEWER
D292
Orang
Eksteenfontein
N7
Goodhouse
Dabenoris
SOUTH AFRICA

Map: Aroab / Ariamsvlei / Augrabies Falls region

Grid C (top)
- **61** (road marker)
- D611, C16, 28, 34
- Löwen
- D578, D612, 21, 22
- D610
- **Aroab** — 26° 48' 02" S, 19° 38' 57" E
- D201, M26, 29, 34, 47
- Warmfontein
- Vredeshoop
- C11
- TARASBERGE / ...ARASBERGE
- D259, D612, 56, 60, 39, 39
- D260
- **Tsaraxaibis** — 27° 24' 58" S, 19° 22' 52" E
- D209, D204, 40, 5, 14, 27
- D258, 32
- C11, D269, D205
- 19, 26, 35, 10, 59, 65
- 37, D251, 8, 23
- 52
- Wolplaas
- Hamab
- **B3**, 56, 17
- Kums
- **Ariamsvlei** — 28° 05' 47" S, 19° 59' 34" E
- D237, Kokerboom
- D202
- C10, 48
- **BLYDEVERWACHT PLATO**
- 35, D211, D202, 11, 26, 65
- D206, 38
- Orange / Kainab
- **Velloorsdrif** — 28° 43' 16" S, 19° 18' 07" E
- 80
- Velloorsdrif
- **VELLOORSDRIF**
- Onseepkans
- (Gariep)
- R358
- Pella
- **N14**, 10, 13, 48

Grid D (right)
- **KLEIN-MENASSE**
- C16, 39
- Rietfontein
- Hakskeenpan
- R31
- D622, 47
- Uitsakpan
- Koopan-Suid
- Obobogorab
- Abiekwasputs
- **HOHLWEG**
- Noenieput
- 28° 05' 47" S, 19° 59' 34" E
- **ARIAMSVLEI**
- Nakop
- **N10**
- Langklip
- 28° 07' 04" S, 19° 50' 26" E
- **Augrabies Falls National Park**
- **Augrabies Falls**
- R64
- Nabies
- Bladgrond
- 64
- **57**

A

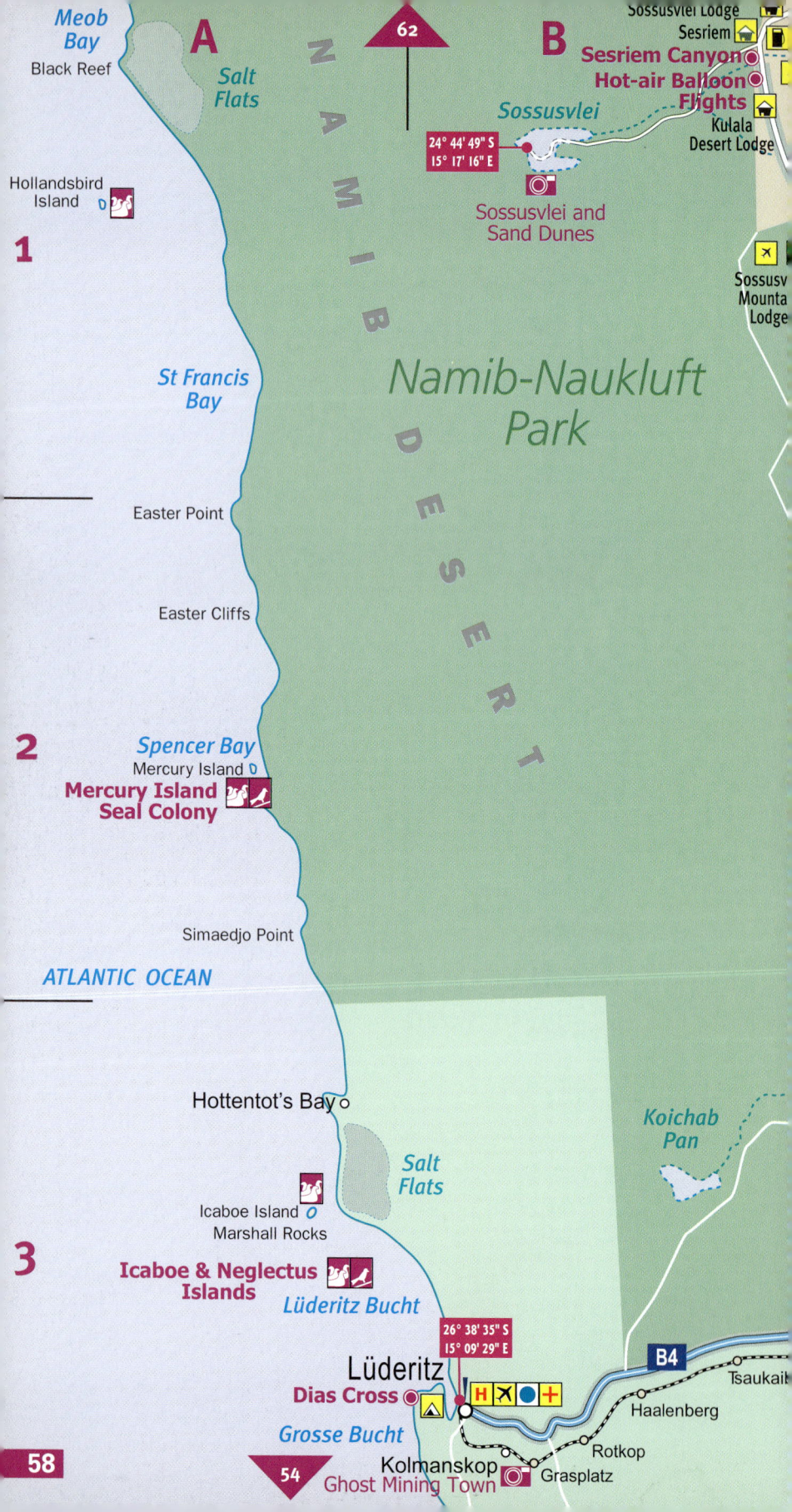

Meob Bay
Black Reef
Salt Flats

Hollandsbird Island

1

St Francis Bay

Easter Point

Easter Cliffs

2

Spencer Bay
Mercury Island
Mercury Island Seal Colony

Simaedjo Point

ATLANTIC OCEAN

Hottentot's Bay

Salt Flats

Icaboe Island
Marshall Rocks

3

Icaboe & Neglectus Islands
Lüderitz Bucht

26° 38' 35" S
15° 09' 29" E

Lüderitz
Dias Cross

Grosse Bucht

Kolmanskop
Ghost Mining Town

B

62

Sossusvlei Lodge
Sesriem
Sesriem Canyon
Hot-air Balloon Flights

Sossusvlei

24° 44' 49" S
15° 17' 16" E

Kulala Desert Lodge

Sossusvlei and Sand Dunes

Sossusv Mountai Lodge

Namib-Naukluft Park

NAMIB DESERT

Koichab Pan

B4
Tsaukaib
Haalenberg
Rotkop
Grasplatz

58   54

C
D
Tsauchab
Fish
63
Zebra River Lodge
Betesda Guest Farm
Sossusvlei Wilderness Camp
TSARISBERGE
1895m
24° 57' 23" S 16° 20' 34" E
24° 52' 40" S 16° 33' 19" E
24° 49' 38" S 17° 06' 53" E
Namseb Game Lodge
Maltahöhe
Hudup
Zaris
Zarishoogte Pass
Grootfontein
Kwisho Camp
Dunes Lodge
Wolwedans Dune Camp
25° 12' 35" S 16° 09' 47" E
25° 15' 42" S 16° 32' 34" E
Duwisib Castle
SCHWARZRAND
69
Namib Rand Nature Reserve
25° 23' 14" S 16° 25' 21" E
Huams
25° 32' 25" S 16° 19' 16" E
Sinclair Guest Farm
ROOIRAND
1920m
25° 53' 26" S 16° 49' 13" E
Helmeringhausen
Mooifontein
Mooifontein Military Cemetery
Great Tiras 1867m
Neisip
View of Neisip Plains
Konkiep
House Schmelen
Bethanie
NO PUBLIC ACCESS
Wild Horses of the Namib
26° 39' 47" S 16° 15' 49" E
Garub
Ausweiche
Aus
Ausnek
Asbospan
Guibes
Goageb
HUIB-HOCH PLATEAU
26° 45' 19" S 17° 13' 40" E
Klein-Aus Vista
Restricted Area (Former Sperrgebiet)
55
59
C14
C19
C21
C27
C13
B4
D854
D850
D845
D831
D861
D827
D830
D826
D808
D804
D811
D813
D1089
D414
D417
D421
D707
D425
D430
D437
D435
D446
D459

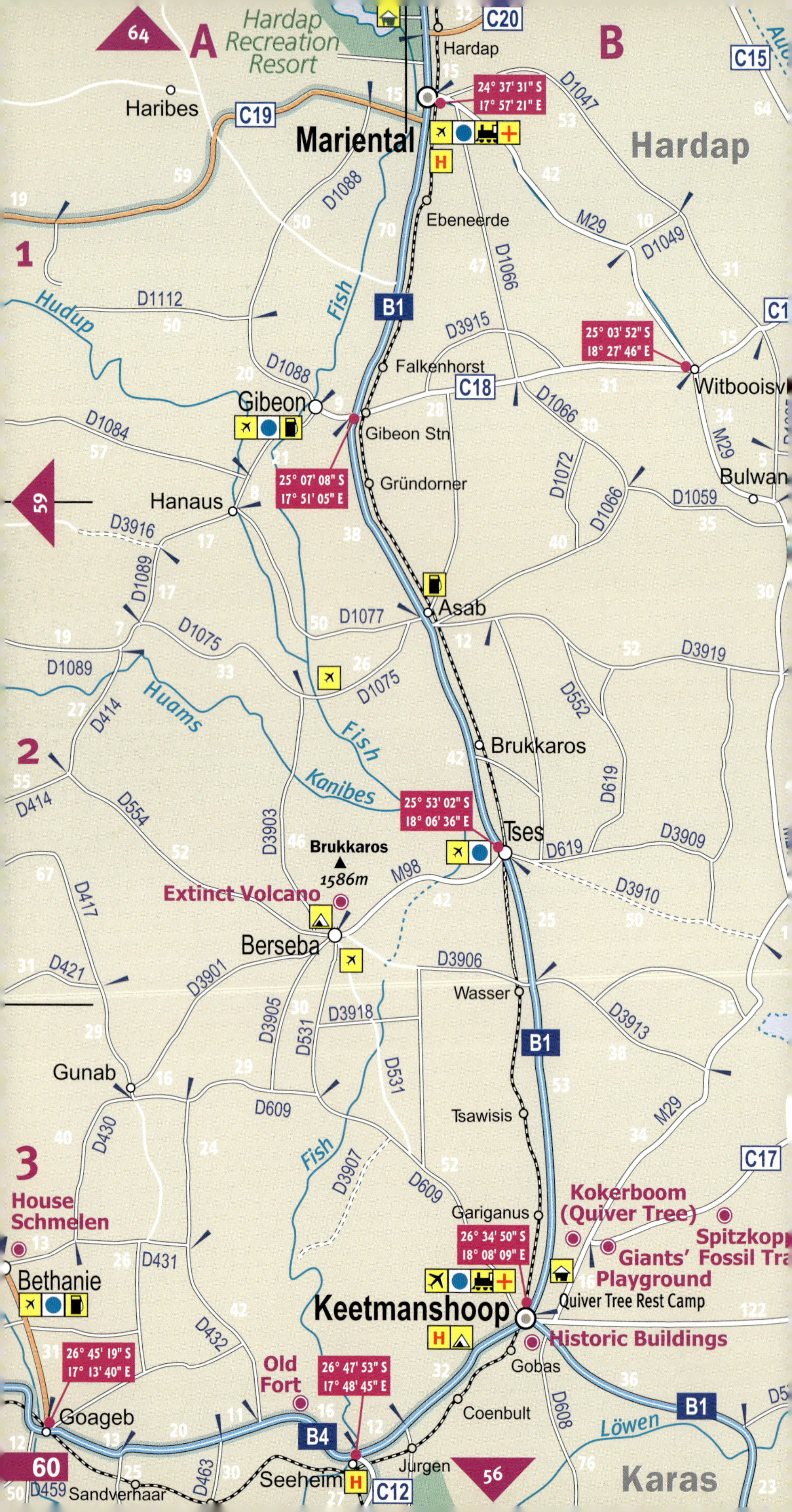

64
A
B
Hardap Recreation Resort
C20
Hardap
C15
Haribes
C19
24° 37' 31" S
17° 57' 21" E
D1047
Mariental
Hardap
D1088
Ebeneerde
M29
D1049
D1066
1
Hudup
D1112
Fish
B1
D3915
25° 03' 52" S
18° 27' 46" E
D1088
Falkenhorst
C18
Witbooisv
Gibeon
D1066
D1084
Gibeon Stn
M29
Gründorner
D1072
Bulwan
59
Hanaus
25° 07' 08" S
17° 51' 05" E
D1066
D1059
D3916
D1089
Asab
D1077
D1075
D3919
D1089
D1075
D552
Huams
D414
Fish
Brukkaros
2
Kanibes
D619
D414
D554
25° 53' 02" S
18° 06' 36" E
Tses
D3903
Brukkaros
1586m
D619
D3909
D417
M98
D3910
Extinct Volcano
Berseba
D421
D3901
D3906
Wasser
D3905
D3918
D3913
D531
B1
Gunab
D531
D609
Tsawisis
M29
D430
Fish
D3907
C17
3
D609
Kokerboom (Quiver Tree)
House Schmelen
Gariganus
Spitzkop
26° 34' 50" S
18° 08' 09" E
Giants' Playground
Fossil Tra
D431
Bethanie
Quiver Tree Rest Camp
Keetmanshoop
D432
Historic Buildings
26° 45' 19" S
17° 13' 40" E
Old Fort
26° 47' 53" S
18° 48' 45" E
Gobas
D608
Goageb
Coenbult
B1
B4
Löwen
60
D463
Jurgen
56
D459
Sandverhaar
Seeheim
C12
Karas

C

65

Nossob

M39
M32
D1053
D1033
D1004
D1078

24° 51' 48" S
18° 48' 16" E

Auob Lodge

M32

Gochas

D1114

24° 38' 49" S
19° 42' 22" E

Akanous

D1114
D1022

NO ENTRY NO EXIT

Union's End

D1032
D1040
D1022

Nossob

Olifants

D1033
D1109

Kgalagadi Transfrontier Park

D617

C15

Eindpaal

D1119

Twee Rivier

D1022

25° 30' 02" S
19° 18' 12" E

D511
D503

C15

D620

D617

C17

Wegdraai

Kalahari Game Lodge

25° 46' 7" S
19° 59' 47" E

NO ENTRY NO EXIT

Welverdiend

Mata Mata

M24

Koës

D616
D503

Auob

R360

25° 56' 21" S
19° 07' 13" E

D611
D615
D616
D503

Garinais

C11

NAMIBIA

SOUTH AFRICA

C16

D611
D612
D610
D578

Löwen

26° 48' 02" S
19° 38' 57" E

KLEIN-MENASSE

Rietfontein

57

Aroab

C11
C16
61

Hakskeenpan

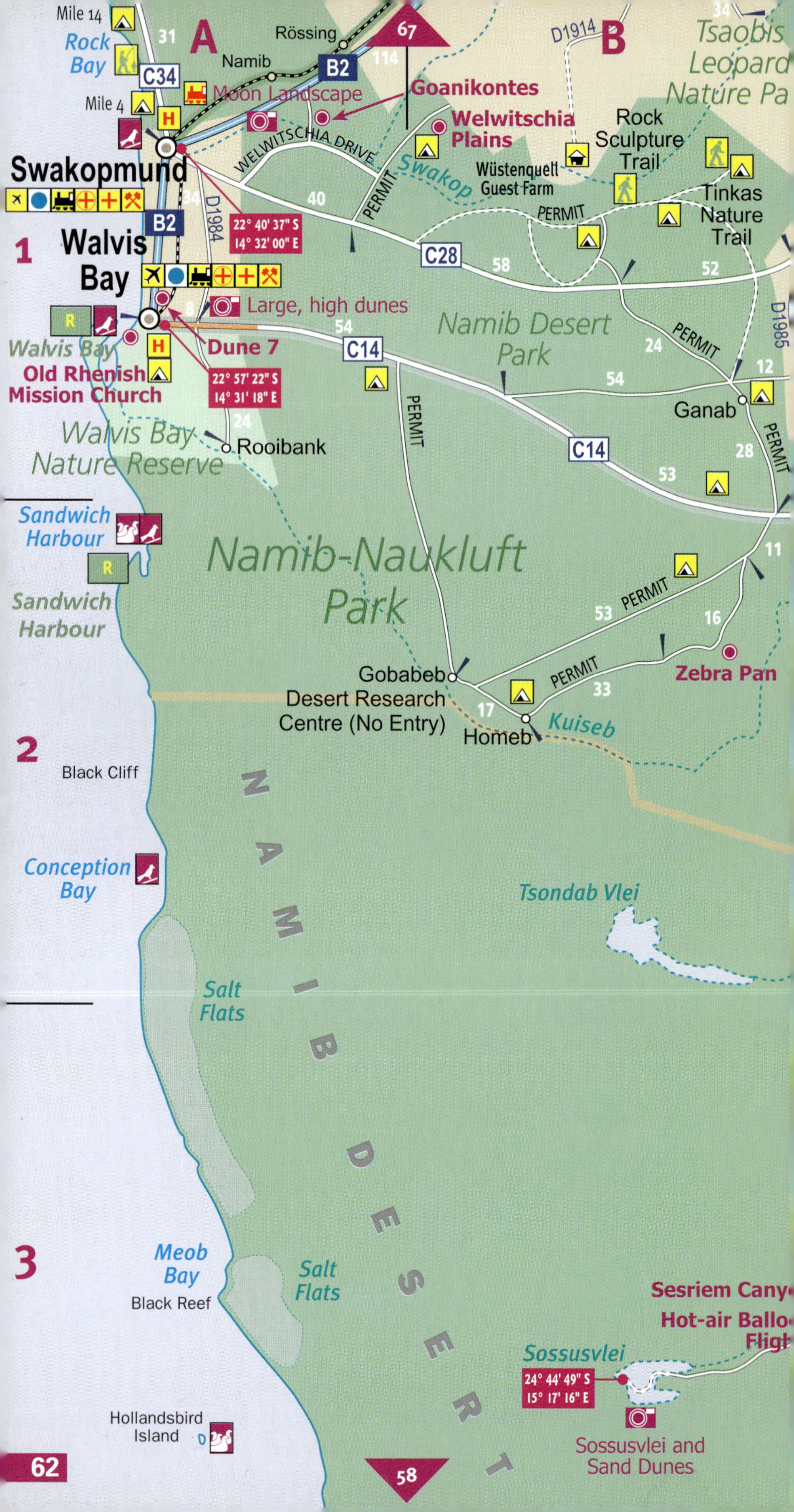

A
B
67
58
1
2
3
Mile 14
Rock Bay
C34
Mile 4
Rössing
Namib
B2
114
Moon Landscape
Goanikontes
Welwitschia Plains
Welwitschia Drive
Swakop
Swakopmund
Walvis Bay
D1984
22° 40' 37" S
14° 32' 00" E
Large, high dunes
Dune 7
22° 57' 22" S
14° 31' 18" E
Walvis Bay
Old Rhenish Mission Church
Walvis Bay Nature Reserve
Rooibank
C14
C28
PERMIT
D1914
Tsaobis Leopard Nature Pa
Rock Sculpture Trail
Wüstenquell Guest Farm
Tinkas Nature Trail
D1985
Namib Desert Park
Ganab
Namib-Naukluft Park
Sandwich Harbour
Gobabeb
Desert Research Centre (No Entry)
Homeb
Kuiseb
Zebra Pan
Black Cliff
Conception Bay
Tsondab Vlei
Salt Flats
NAMIB DESERT
Meob Bay
Black Reef
Sesriem Cany
Hot-air Ballo Fligh
Sossusvlei
24° 44' 49" S
15° 17' 16" E
Sossusvlei and Sand Dunes
Hollandsbird Island

Namibia Map — Khomas Hochland / Naukluft Region

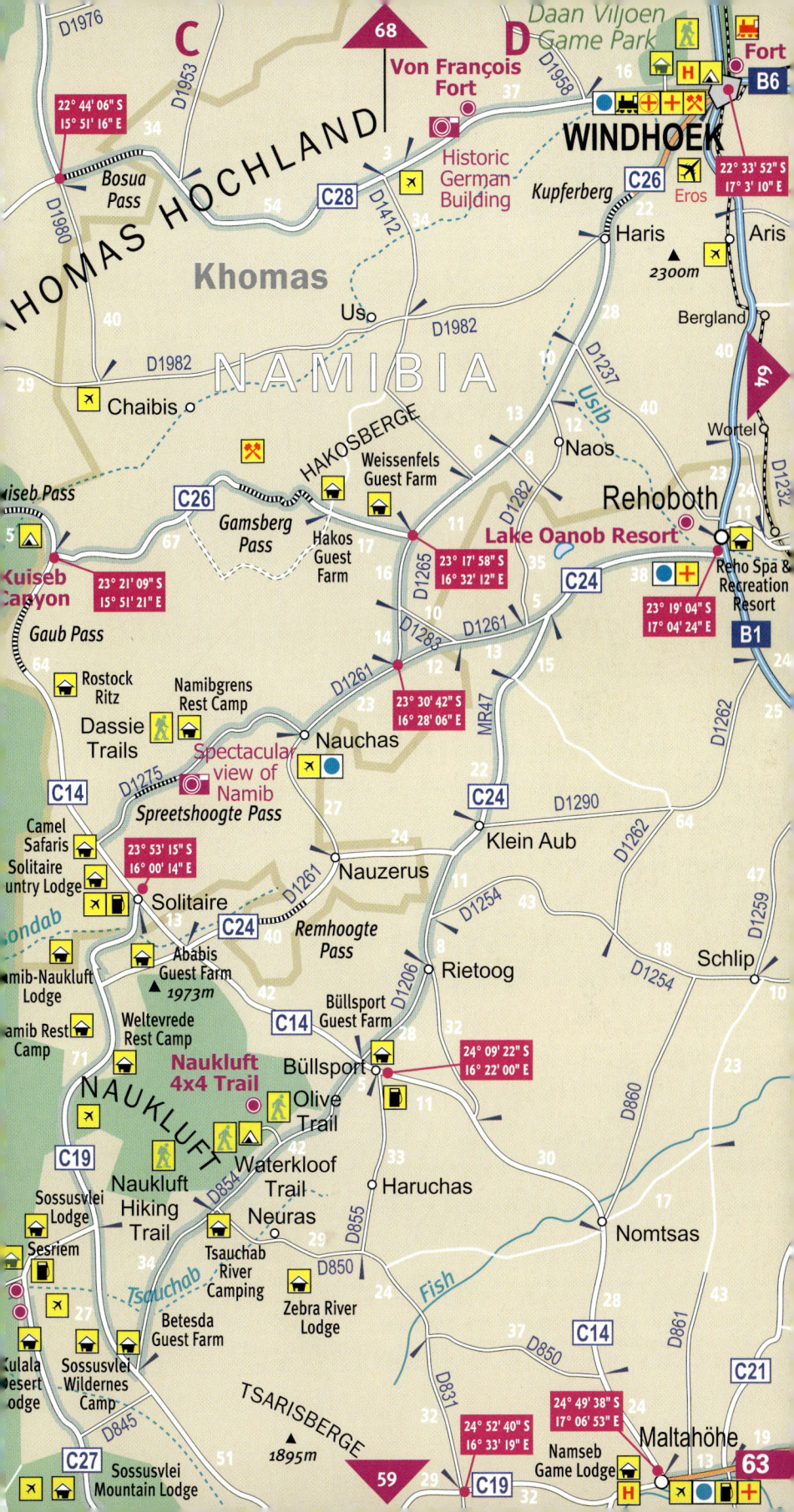

Grid C / D — Reference 68

Windhoek area
- Von François Fort
- Historic German Building
- Daan Viljoen Game Park
- Fort
- Eros
- Kupferberg
- Haris
- Aris (2300m)
- Bergland

Coordinates:
- 22° 44' 06" S / 15° 51' 16" E (Bosua Pass)
- 22° 33' 52" S / 17° 3' 10" E (Windhoek/Eros)

Roads: D1976, D1953, D1980, D1958, B6, C28, D1412, C26

Khomas / Namibia

- Chaibis
- Us
- Hakosberge
- Weissenfels Guest Farm
- Gamsberg Pass
- Hakos Guest Farm
- Naos
- Rehoboth
- Lake Oanob Resort
- Wortel
- Reho Spa & Recreation Resort

Coordinates:
- 23° 21' 09" S / 15° 51' 21" E (Kuiseb Canyon)
- 23° 17' 58" S / 16° 32' 12" E
- 23° 19' 04" S / 17° 04' 24" E

Roads: D1982, D1237, D1265, D1282, D1283, D1261, C24, B1, D1233

Reference: 64

Kuiseb Pass / Gaub Pass area

- Kuiseb Canyon
- Gaub Pass
- Rostock Ritz
- Dassie Trails
- Namibgrens Rest Camp
- Nauchas
- Spectacular view of Namib
- Spreetshoogte Pass
- Camel Safaris
- Solitaire Country Lodge
- Solitaire
- Ababis Guest Farm (1973m)
- Remhoogte Pass
- Nauzerus
- Klein Aub
- Rietoog
- Schlip
- Büllsport Guest Farm
- Büllsport

Coordinates:
- 23° 30' 42" S / 16° 28' 06" E
- 23° 53' 15" S / 16° 00' 14" E
- 24° 09' 22" S / 16° 22' 00" E

Roads: C14, D1275, D1261, C24, MR47, D1290, D1262, D1254, D1259, D1206, D860

Naukluft area

- Namib-Naukluft Lodge
- Namib Rest Camp
- Weltevrede Rest Camp
- Naukluft 4x4 Trail
- Naukluft Hiking Trail
- Olive Trail
- Waterkloof Trail
- Neuras
- Tsauchab River Camping
- Zebra River Lodge
- Haruchas
- Nomtsas
- Betesda Guest Farm
- Sossusvlei Lodge
- Sesriem
- Kulala Desert Lodge
- Sossusvlei Wilderness Camp
- Sossusvlei Mountain Lodge
- Namseb Game Lodge
- Maltahöhe

Tsarisberge (1895m)

Coordinates:
- 24° 52' 40" S / 16° 33' 19" E
- 24° 49' 38" S / 17° 06' 53" E

Roads: C19, D854, D855, D850, D831, D845, D861, C14, C21, C27

Rivers: Tsauchab, Fish

References: 59, 63

Heja Game Lodge
Finkenstein
Kapp's Farm
Ondekaremba
A
B
B6
69
M51
D1472
D1808
D1800
Okasewa
D1801
D1793
Arnhem Cave
D1792
D1444
D1785
Doreenville
Auasberge
2479m
C23
Brack
D1463
1
Auas Game Lodge
D1249
Skaap
D1482
Dordabis
Bergland
C15
C23
Nina
M51
D1790
D1423
Garib
Wortel
D1232
D1228
Rehoboth
Girib
Klein Nauas
D1223
C23
D1248
63
C25
Gebied
Usib
Heide
D1219
C15
B1
D1230
C25
D1218
C25
Derm
D1775
2
D1230
Tsumis Park
Uhlenhorst
D1212
D1215
D1259
D1222
C41
D1318
Duineveld
D1264
D1215
D1239
C21
D1268
Schlip
Kalkrand
C15
Lidfontein
24° 04' 17" S
17° 35' 20" E
Narib
Intu Afrika
Eirup
Fish
Twilight
C41
Stampriet
Salzbrunn
C21
C20
Hardap Recreation Resort
Anib Lodge
24° 20' 53" S
18° 25' 00" E
3
24° 37' 31" S
17° 57' 21" E
Hardap
D1047
Haribes
C19
Mariental
Hardap
D1088
D1066
Fish
Ebeneerde
M29
D1049
64
60
B1

Gobabis
C
D
70
1530m
C20
22° 26' 25" S
18° 58' 39" E
Kakus
D1707
D1681
D1805
D1700
Swart-Nossob
Wit-Nossob
Keitsas
C22
D1604
D1715
D1716
D1734
D1793
D1790
D1837
D1718
C20
Hoaseb
Onderombapa
D3819
D3820
M40
Gross Ums
D1715
D3821
D1782
C23
Leonardville
D3815
C22
Motsomi
M40
D1770
Aminuis
D1004
D3817
D1765
Nossob
D3820
D1775
C42
D1001
D1001
Vogelweide
C22
D1046
24° 10' 10" S
19° 06' 41" E
D1010
D1010
C20
Aranos
D1042
C20
D1004
D1046
D1043
D1052
D1016
D1099
D1041
M39
D1004
D1053
D1078
24° 38' 49" S
19° 42' 22" E
Akanous
D1033
M32
NO ENTRY
NO EXIT
24° 51' 48" S
18° 48' 16" E
D1114
D1114
D1022
Auob Lodge
C18
Gochas
61
Union's End

Skeleton Coast Park

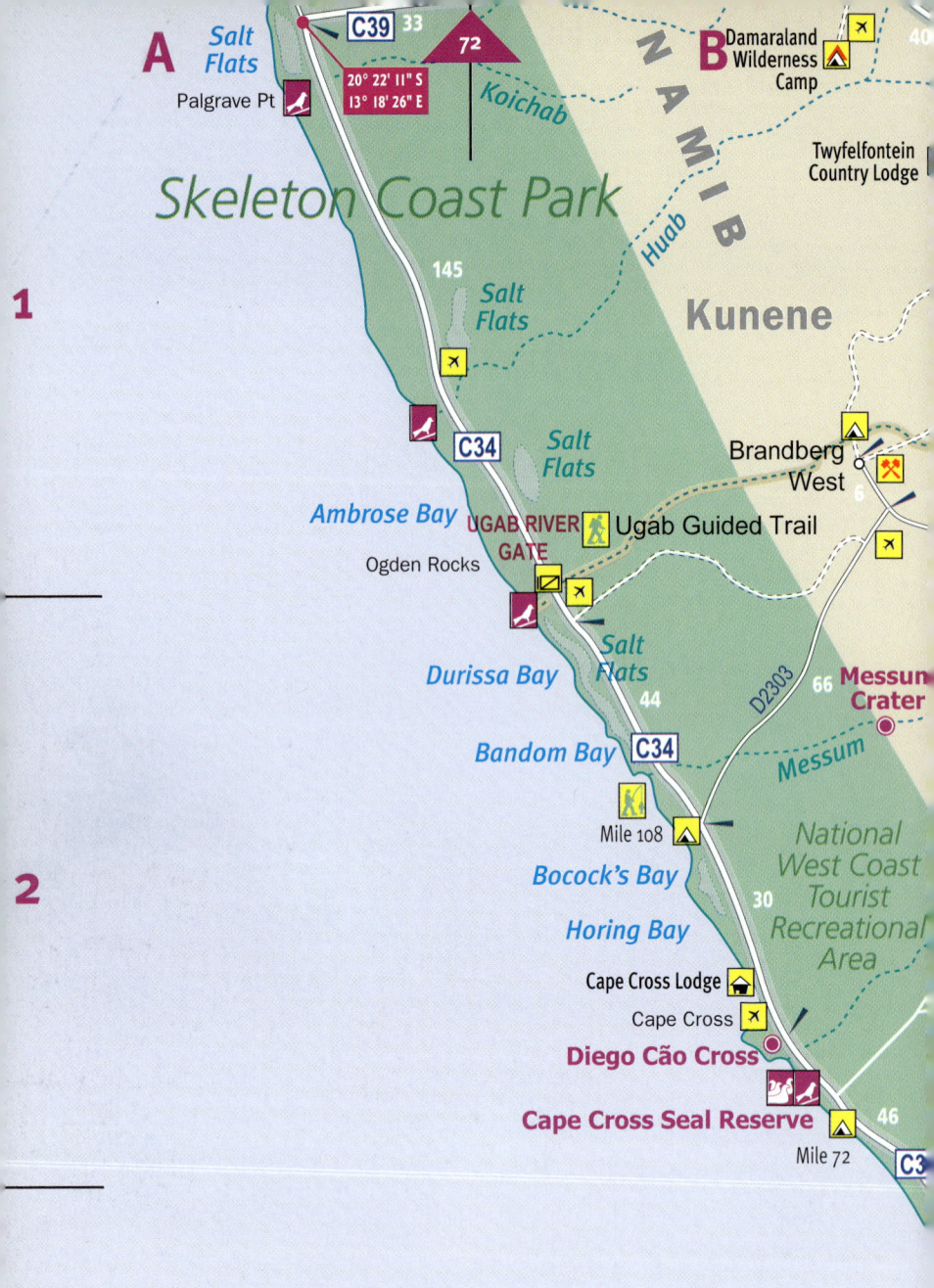

A Salt Flats
Palgrave Pt
C39 33
20° 22' 11" S
13° 18' 26" E
72
Koichab

B Damaraland Wilderness Camp
Twyfelfontein Country Lodge

Huab

145
Salt Flats

Kunene

C34
Salt Flats

Brandberg West

Ambrose Bay
UGAB RIVER GATE
Ugab Guided Trail
Ogden Rocks

Durissa Bay
Salt Flats
44
D2303 66
Messum Crater

Bandom Bay
C34
Messum

Mile 108

Bocock's Bay
National West Coast Tourist Recreational Area

Horing Bay
30

Cape Cross Lodge
Cape Cross
Diego Cão Cross
Cape Cross Seal Reserve
Mile 72
46
C3

ATLANTIC OCEAN

66

Map: Erongo / Namib-Naukluft region (Namibia)

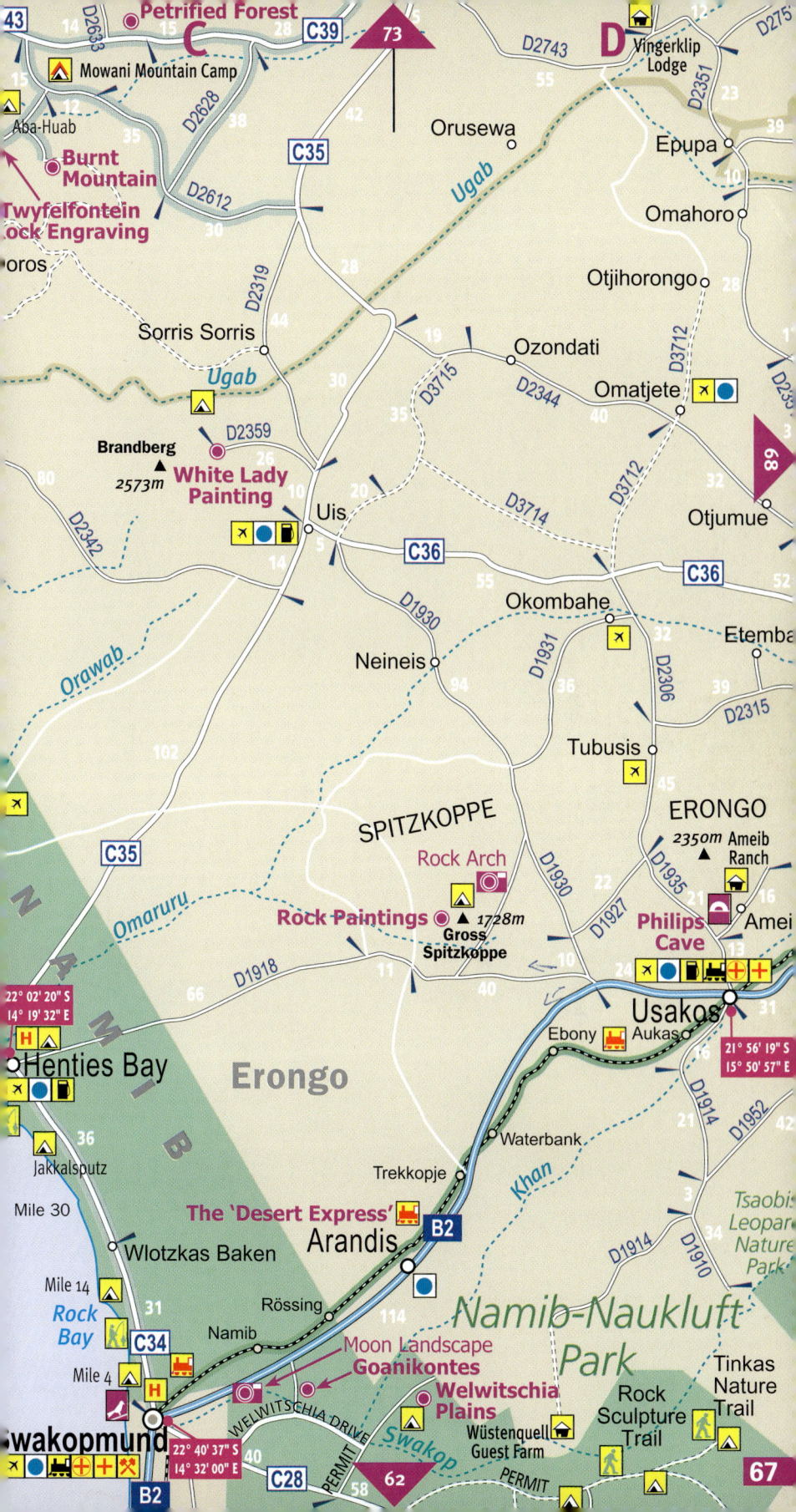

Labels and place names

- **Petrified Forest** (C)
- Mowani Mountain Camp
- Aba-Huab
- **Burnt Mountain**
- **Twyfelfontein Rock Engraving**
- oros
- Sorris Sorris
- Ugab
- Brandberg 2573m
- **White Lady Painting**
- Uis
- Orusewa
- Ozondati
- Omatjete
- Otjumue
- Okombahe
- Etemba
- Neineis
- Tubusis
- **SPITZKOPPE**
- Rock Arch
- **Rock Paintings**
- Gross Spitzkoppe 1728m
- **ERONGO** — Ameib Ranch 2350m
- **Philips Cave**
- Amei
- Usakos
- Ebony
- Aukas
- **Henties Bay**
- Jakkalsputz
- Mile 30
- Mile 14
- Rock Bay
- Mile 4
- **wakopmund** (Swakopmund)
- Wlotzkas Baken
- **The 'Desert Express'**
- **Arandis**
- Rössing
- Namib
- Waterbank
- Trekkopje
- **Moon Landscape** — **Goanikontes**
- **Welwitschia Plains**
- Wüstenquell Guest Farm
- Tinkas Nature Trail
- Rock Sculpture Trail
- Tsaobis Leopard Nature Park
- **Namib-Naukluft Park**
- Erongo
- Vingerklip Lodge (D)
- Epupa
- Omahoro
- Otjihorongo

Rivers
- Ugab
- Orawab
- Omaruru
- Khan
- Swakop

Roads
- B2, C28, C34, C35, C36, C39, D2612, D2628, D2633, D2319, D2342, D2344, D2351, D2743, D275, D2306, D2315, D2359, D3712, D3714, D3715, D1910, D1914, D1918, D1927, D1930, D1931, D1935, D1952, 43

Coordinates
- 22° 02' 20" S, 14° 19' 32" E
- 21° 56' 19" S, 15° 50' 57" E
- 22° 40' 37" S, 14° 32' 00" E

Page references
- 73
- 68
- 67
- 62

NAMIB

A
B
1
2
3
74
67
63
Otjiwarongo
Heuningberg
Otjitasu
D2505
C38
20° 27' 57" S
16° 38' 59" E
20° 39' 45" S
16° 57' 29" E
Otjibamba Lodge
B1
C22
Ozondjache
C30
D2417
D2418
D2403
C33
Erundu
D2515
D2511
Otjiwa Lodge
Avond
D2493
Kameelberg
Okonjima
Kalkveld
Eremutua
D2339
D2338
D2351
D2414
Mt Etjo Safari Lodge
D2483
21° 02' 09" S
16° 49' 18" E
Kaalkop
Otuwe
D2334
Dinosaur's Footprints
Sukses
Otjumue
Tjirundo
Ondumbo
Etjo
D2404
Evero
Omatako
Epako Game Lodge
Okozangoro
D2329
D2344
Epako
D2328
D2187
Okakombo
C36
Omaruru Game Lodge
Etemba
D2315
Omaruru
21° 24' 57" S
15° 57' 33" E
D2112
Erongo Wilderness Lodge
Norman
D2414
D2121
D2108
D2110
Otjisemba
D2180
Oropoko Lodge
D2110
Erongo
Otjimbovo
D1941
Etiro
Ombo Ostrich Farm
Okahandja Lodge
D2756
Albrechts
Vogelsang
Okazize
D2102
Waldau
Karibib
Wilhelmstal
B2
Etusis Lodge
D1992
D1967
Ozombando Guest Farm
Okahandja
D1952
Komitundu Guest Farm
D2192
M87
21° 58' 58" S
16° 54' 53" E
Hot Springs
Gross Barmen
Teufelsbach
D1953
D1958
Swakop
D1967
D1972
B1
C32
Otjihajavara
Düsternbrook Guest Farm
Otjimbingwe
Powder Tower
Okapuka Lodge
D1976
D1958
Brakwater
Sweet Thorn Hiking Trail
Tsaobis Leopard Nature Park
Daan Viljoen Game Park
D1953
Von François Fort
KHOMAS HOCHLAND
WINDHOEK
22° 44' 06" S
15° 51' 16" E
Bosua Pass
Historic German Building
Eros
Kupferberg
C26
D1980
C28
D1414
Khomas
22° 33' 52"
17° 3' 10" E
Haris

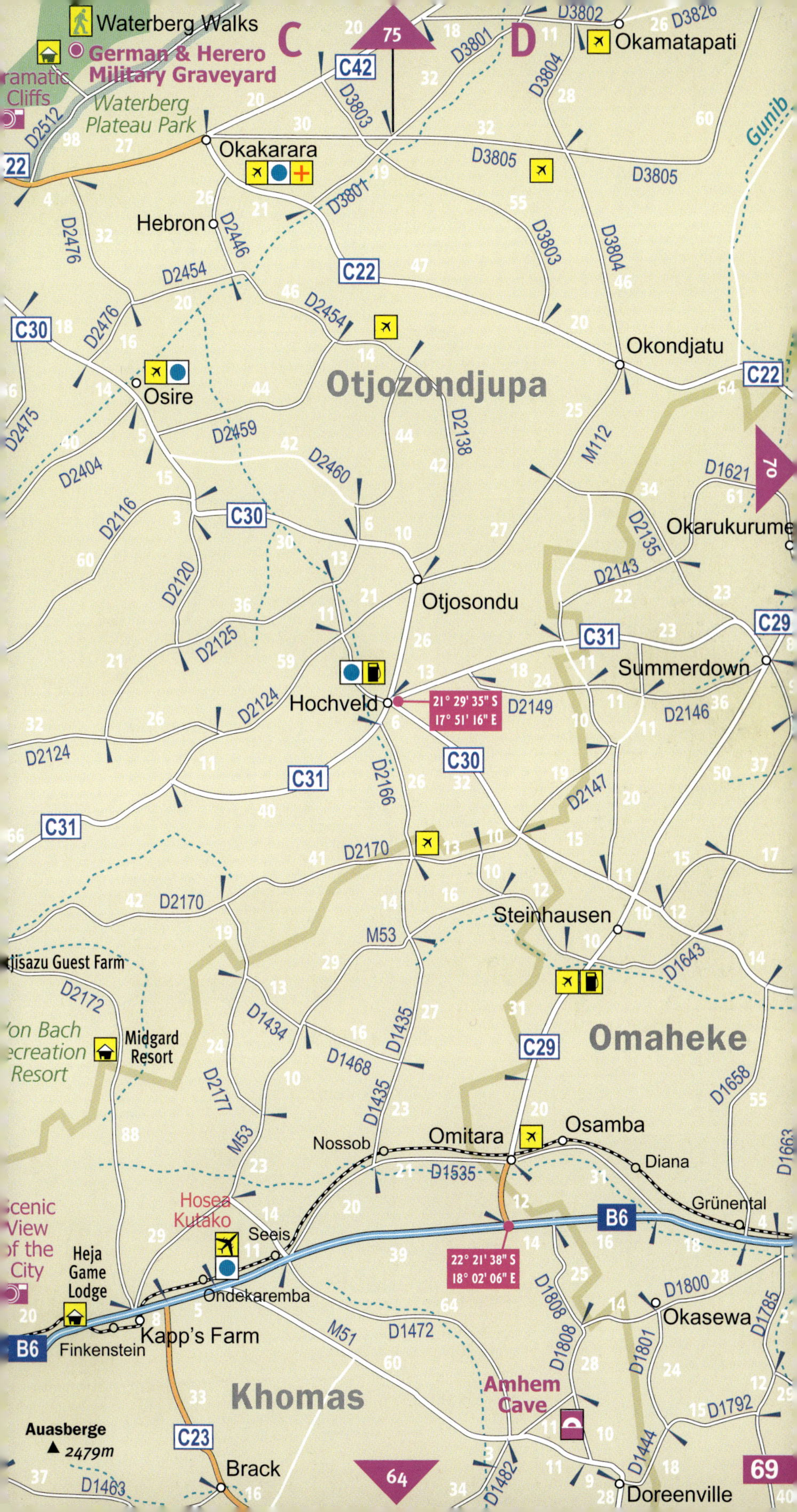

Waterberg Walks
German & Herero Military Graveyard
Waterberg Plateau Park
Dramatic Cliffs
Okakarara
Okamatapati
Hebron
Osire
Otjozondjupa
Okondjatu
Okarukurume
Otjosondu
Summerdown
Hochveld
21° 29' 35" S 17° 51' 16" E
Steinhausen
Omaheke
Ojisazu Guest Farm
Von Bach Recreation Resort
Midgard Resort
Nossob
Omitara
Osamba
Diana
Grünental
Hosea Kutako
Seeis
Scenic View of the City
Heja Game Lodge
Ondekaremba
Finkenstein
Kapp's Farm
22° 21' 38" S 18° 02' 06" E
Okasewa
Arnhem Cave
Khomas
Auasberge 2479m
Brack
Doreenville
Gunib
C42
C22
C30
C31
C29
C23
B6
M112
M53
M51
D3802
D3826
D3801
D3803
D3804
D3805
D2512
D2476
D2446
D2454
D2475
D2459
D2460
D2138
D2404
D2116
D2120
D2125
D2124
D2135
D2143
D1621
D2149
D2146
D2166
D2147
D2170
D1643
D2172
D1434
D1468
D1435
D2177
D1658
D1535
D1663
D1800
D1808
D1785
D1472
D1801
D1792
D1444
D1482
D1463
75
70
64
C
D

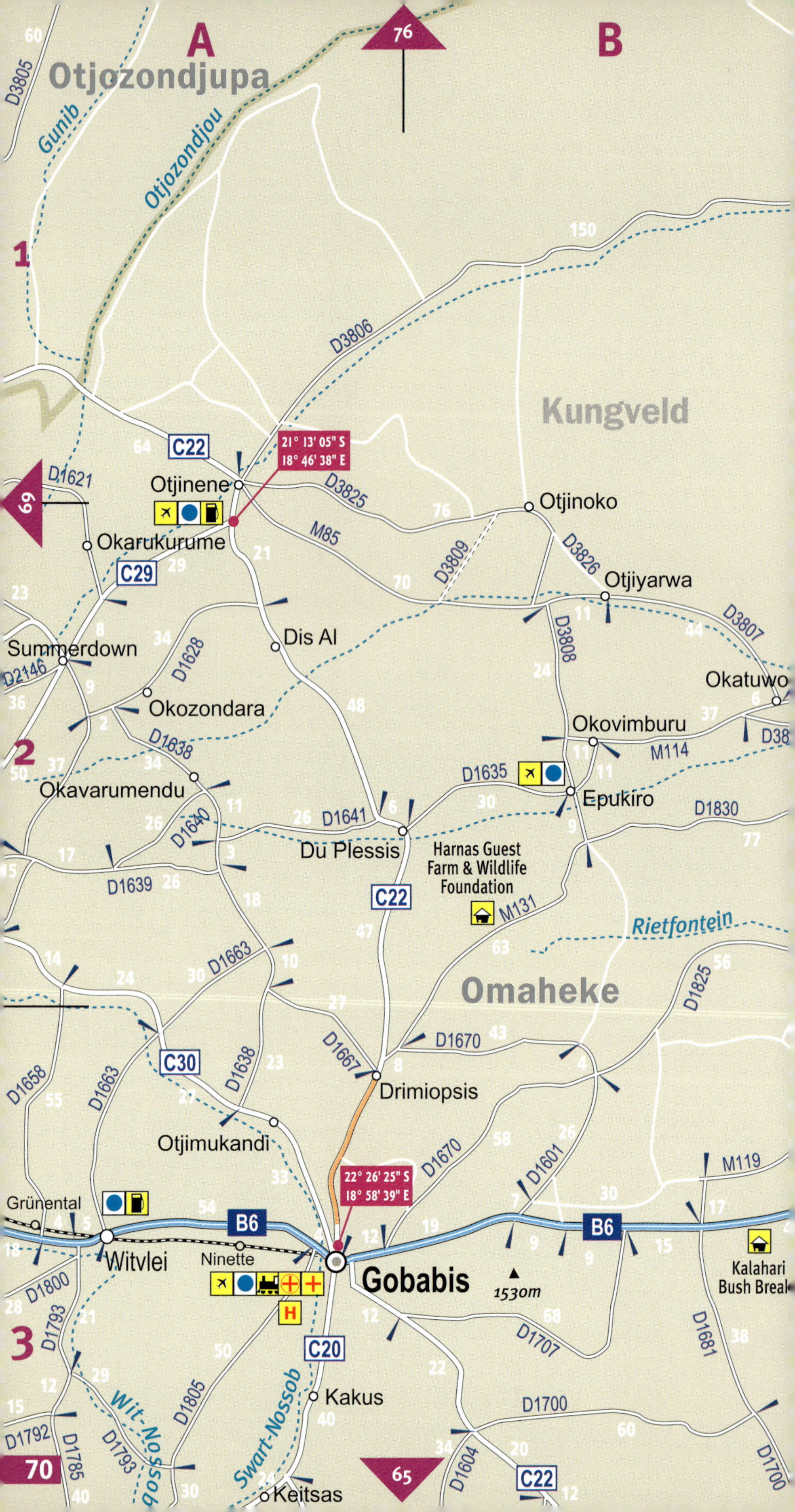
A
B
1
2
3
76
69
65
Otjozondjupa
Kungveld
Omaheke
Gunib
Otjozondjou
Rietfontein
Wit-Nossob
Swart-Nossob
C22
C29
C30
C20
B6
M85
M114
M131
M119
D3805
D3806
D3825
D3809
D3826
D3808
D3807
D1621
D1628
D2146
D1638
D1640
D1641
D1635
D1830
D1639
D1663
D1667
D1670
D1825
D1658
D1601
D1800
D1793
D1805
D1707
D1681
D1700
D1792
D1785
D1604
21° 13' 05" S
18° 46' 38" E
22° 26' 25" S
18° 58' 39" E
Otjinene
Okarukurume
Otjinoko
Otjiyarwa
Summerdown
Dis Al
Okozondara
Okatuwo
Okovimburu
Okavarumendu
Epukiro
Du Plessis
Harnas Guest
Farm & Wildlife
Foundation
Drimiopsis
Otjimukandi
Grünental
Witvlei
Ninette
Gobabis
1530m
Kalahari
Bush Break
Kakus
Keitsas

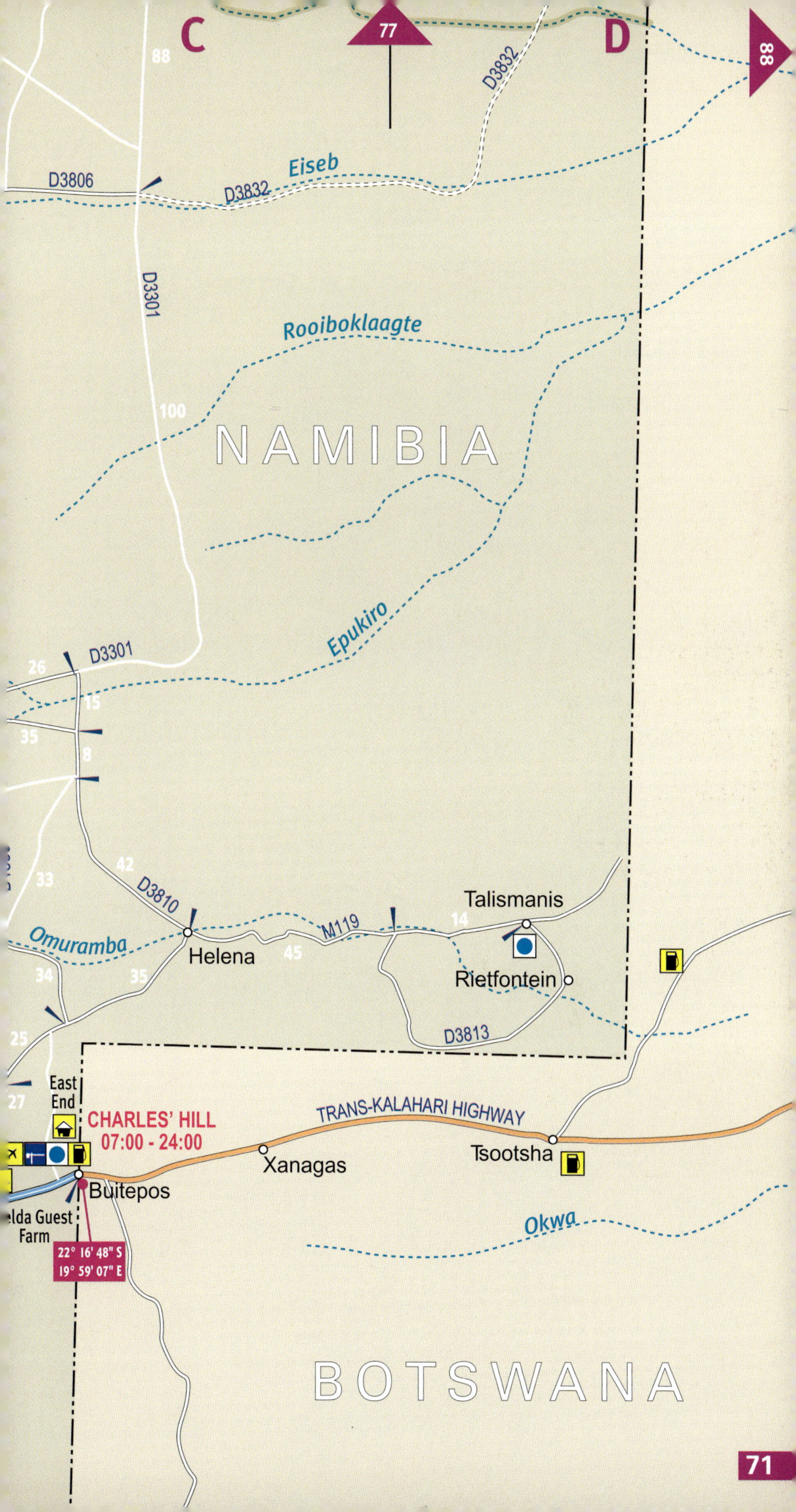
C
D
77
88
88
D3832
D3806
Eiseb
D3832
D3301
Rooiboklaagte
100
NAMIBIA
Epukiro
D3301
26
15
35
8
33
42
D3810
Omuramba
Helena
45
M119
14
Talismanis
Rietfontein
34
35
D3813
25
27
East End
CHARLES' HILL
07:00 - 24:00
TRANS-KALAHARI HIGHWAY
Xanagas
Tsootsha
Buitepos
Zelda Guest Farm
22° 16' 48" S
19° 59' 07" E
Okwa
BOTSWANA

Map: Kaokoland / Kunene / Skeleton Coast Park

Grid columns: A, B
Grid rows: 1, 2, 3

Places and features

- Okandjombo
- Oruwanje
- Kaoko Otavi — C43
- D3707, D3705, D3710, D3709
- **79** (page reference)
- **Kaokoland**
- **JOUBERTBERGE**
- Otjitoko
- Robbie's Pass
- Okatumba
- Ombombo
- Otjondek
- 18° 41' 45" S / 14° 15' 26" E
- Otjikondavirongo
- D3708
- Otjitunduwa
- **Dorslandtrekkers Monument**
- Purros
- Tomakas
- Ganamub
- Otjitaimo
- Otjomatemba
- C43
- D3710
- 18° 43' 15" S / 13° 55' 19" E
- **78**
- Ganamub
- Sesfontein
- **Old Fort**
- Fort Sesfontein
- **Blinkwater Falls**
- Warmquelle
- D3106
- Khowarib
- Baadjie
- 19° 07' 32" S / 13° 37' 01" E
- Hoanib
- Dubis
- Ombonde
- Amspoort
- **NO ENTRY**
- **Kunene**
- C43
- **Skeleton Coast Park**
- NO PUBLIC ACCESS
- NAMIB
- 19° 54' 41" S / 13° 59' 12" E
- **Etendeka Mountain Camp**
- Palmwag Lodge
- Palmwag
- C40
- Grootberg Pass
- Terrace Bay
- Uniab
- 19° 57' 22" S / 13° 56' 15" E
- Dune Point
- C34
- Shallow Breakers
- C43
- Wereldsend
- 20° 14' 37" S / 14° 02' 08" E
- Bergsig
- Torra Bay
- C39
- **SPRINGBOK WASSER GATE**
- Salt Flats
- 20° 22' 11" S / 13° 18' 26" E
- Palgrave Pt
- C34
- Koichab
- **Damaraland Wilderness Camp**
- Huab
- **Twyfelfontein Country Lodge**
- **Twyfelfontein Rock Engravir**
- **72**
- **66**
- 145

State Forest

Natukanaoka Pan

Western area of park open to registered tour operators only

Etosha National Park

Duineveld *Nomab* *Tobieroen* *Sonderkop* *Ozonjuitji m'Bari*
Dolomietpunt *Teespoed* *Duiwelsvuur*
Rateldraf *Okawao* *Charl Marais Pan*
Aasvoëlbad *Jakkalswater*

Toilet
Moringa Forest

19° 19' 56" S
14° 22' 13" E

Otjovasandu

obatere Lodge

Gagarus
Mon Desir

Weissbrünn
Rock Engravings
Biermanskool

Kamanjab
19° 39' 22" S
14° 49' 23" E
Otjitambi

Grootberg
Otjikondo

Huab Lodge
Tutara
Cauas

Fransfontein
FRANSFONTEIN MTS
1553m

Khorixas Rest Camp
Gainatseb

Petrified Forest
Khorixas
Vingerklip (Rock Finger)
Vingerklip Lodge

Mowani Mountain Camp
20° 22' 10" S
15° 02' 26" E

20° 23' 36" S
15° 25' 47" E

Burnt Mountain
Orusewa
Epupa

A
B
1
2
3
81
73
68
B1
NEHALE LYA MPINGANA GATE
Andoni
Toilet
Cuvelai and Etosha Pan
Natukanaoka Pan
Etosha Pan
Groot Okevi
Historic Fort
LINDEQU
Klein Okevi
Namutoni
Okerfontein
C38
Springbokfontein
Chudob
Okondeka
Rietfontein
Halali
Kalkheuwel
19° 10' 44" S
15° 55' 10" E
Moringa Forest
Okaukuejo
Aus
Etosha National Park
ANDERSSON GATE
Ongava Lodge
D2695
D2779
Toshari Inn
D2865
D2782
C39
19° 35' 34" S
15° 52' 41" E
D2710
D2873
D2780
D2761
D2696
Gamkarab Cave
Neina
D2869
D2886
Goreis
C40
Nugubaes
20° 06' 06" S
16° 08' 23" E
Outjo
D2775
D2468
Okaput
Vrindskap
D2773
M63
Otjikang
Ugab
Hartseer
D2433
Okave
20° 27' 57" S
16° 38' 59" E
D2430
Otjenga
D2752
Heuningberg
Otjiwarongo
Otjitasu
D2427
D2505
C33
Otjibamba Lodge
20° 39' 45" S
16° 57' 29" E
D2477
D2418
D2515
Erundu
Ozondjach
D3605

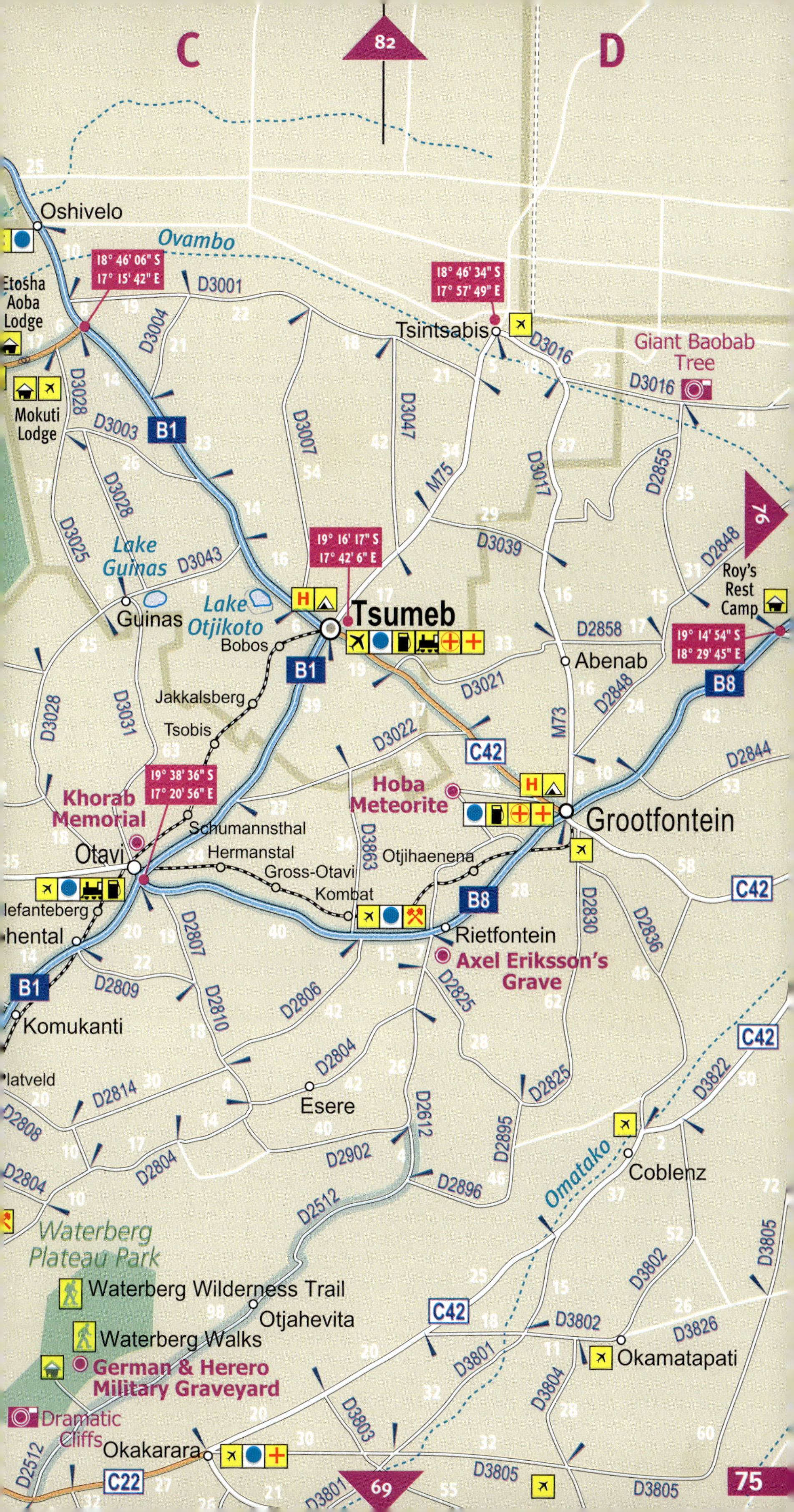

C
D
82
Oshivelo
Ovambo
18° 46' 06" S
17° 15' 42" E
Etosha Aoba Lodge
D3001
D3004
Mokuti Lodge
D3028
D3003
B1
18° 46' 34" S
17° 57' 49" E
Tsintsabis
D3016
Giant Baobab Tree
D3016
D3007
D3047
M75
D3017
D2855
76
D3028
D3025
Lake Guinas
D3043
Lake Otjikoto
19° 16' 17" S
17° 42' 6" E
Tsumeb
D3039
D2848
Roy's Rest Camp
19° 14' 54" S
18° 29' 45" E
Guinas
Bobos
D2858
Abenab
B1
D3021
D2848
B8
D3028
D3031
Jakkalsberg
Tsobis
D3022
C42
M73
D2844
19° 38' 36" S
17° 20' 56" E
Khorab Memorial
Hoba Meteorite
Grootfontein
Schumannsthal
Otavi
Hermanstal
D3863
Otjihaenena
Gross-Otavi
Kombat
B8
Rietfontein
D2830
D2836
C42
lefanteberg
hental
D2807
Axel Eriksson's Grave
D2825
B1
D2809
D2810
D2806
Komukanti
C42
D2804
D2825
latveld
D2814
Esere
D3822
D2808
D2612
D2895
D2804
D2902
Coblenz
D2804
D2896
Omatako
D2512
Waterberg Plateau Park
D3805
D3802
Waterberg Wilderness Trail
Otjahevita
C42
D3802
D3826
Waterberg Walks
D3801
Okamatapati
German & Herero Military Graveyard
D3804
D3803
Dramatic Cliffs
Okakarara
D2512
C22
D3801
69
D3805
D3805

Map: Otjozondjupa region, Namibia

Grid: A, B / 1, 2, 3

Major roads & markers:
- B8 (150)
- ▲ 83
- ◄ 75

Towns and places:
- Mangetti
- Mururani
- Maanlig
- Karakuwisa
- Roy's Rest Camp
- Maroelaboom
- Kano Vlei
- Luhebu
- Otjituuo

Coordinates marker:
19° 14' 54" S
18° 29' 45" E

Roads (D/C/B numbers):
- D3016
- D2908
- D2848
- D2898
- D2845
- D2868
- D2874
- D2893
- D2844
- D2803
- D3800
- D3306
- D3822
- D3805
- D3826
- C44
- C42
- B8

Distances (km) shown along roads:
28, 12, 18, 30, 22, 39, 14, 31, 28, 23, 32, 16, 21, 27, 43, 8, 44, 42, 53, 14, 23, 14, 26, 36, 3, 5, 6, 8, 15, 50, 72, 60, 114

Rivers:
- Omatako
- Otjozondjou
- Gunib

Region: Otjozondjupa

Country: NAMIBIA

▼ 70

C | D

84

18° 35' 39" S
20° 33' 45" E

Tamsu

Khaudum

Khaudum

Nxamasere

Doringstraat Waterhole

Khaudum Game Park

Elands Drink Waterhole

Dussi Waterhole

Nhoma

Sikereti

Soncana Waterhole

BOTSWANA

88

Samagaigai

D3403

D3309

Nhoma

Nhoma

D3312

D3303

D3311

D3303

D3309

Dorsland Trek Baobab

Aasvoëlnes

Klein Dobe

19° 35' 35" S
20° 30' 22" E

C44

27

29

14

Tsumkwe Lodge

Tsumkwe

Holboom

Djokwe

Holboom

Makuri

Grootboom (Giant Baobab Tree)

M74

DOBE

14

Quankwa

31

35

Caecae (Xaixai)

D3301

37

D3302

42

Tweeputte

D3300

D3303

Nama Pan

C44

9

27

Gcwihaba (Drotsky's) Cave

Daneib

88

Gam

D3806

D3832

Eiseb

71

77

A　　　　　　B

1

Serra Cafema Lodge

Cunene

Otjinungwa

17° 14' 50" S
12° 25' 09" E

HARTMANN MTS

OTJIHIPA MTS

17° 28' 04" S
13° 03' 41" E

Etengw

17° 33' 18" S
12° 33' 14" E

17° 37' 25" S
12° 51' 29" E

D3703

Okau

Otjitan

Van Zyl's Pass

Salt Flats

NO ENTRY

17° 47' 49" S
12° 31' 22" E

17° 39' 20" S
12° 41' 43" E

17° 46' 5
12° 57' 4

NO ENTRY

17° 47' 23" S
12° 23' 20" E

2

NO ENTRY

Salt Flats

Orupembe

18° 04' 18" S
12° 44' 29" E

18° 09' 22" S
12° 33' 38" E

Sanitatas

Okandjom

Cape Fria

ETENDEKA

NO ENTRY

Public Access Restricted

Skeleton Coast Camp

NO ENTRY

Purros

3

Rocky Point

Skeleton Coast Park

Hoarusib

ATLANTIC OCEAN

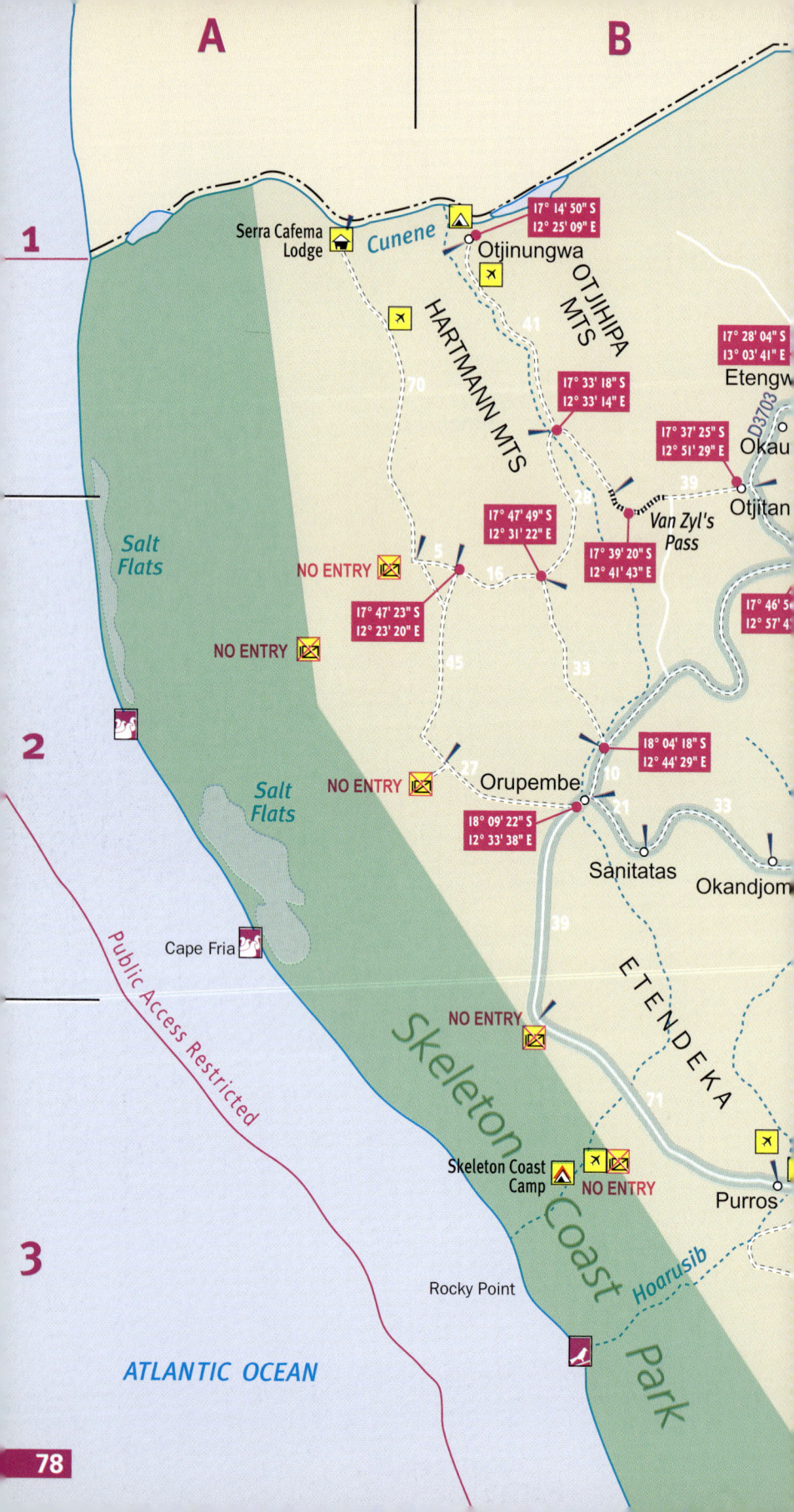

78

C

pupa Falls
Dramatic Waterfall

17° 00' 09" S
13° 14' 39" E

C43

17° 13' 40" S
13° 14' 11" E

Enyandi

ZEBRA MTS

D3700

17° 20' 28" S
13° 50' 56" E

17° 26' 01" S
13° 16' 20" E

Omuhonga

Swartbooisdrift

Okangwati

Ondoto

Otjijandjasemo Hot Spring

Epembe

Otjiveze

17° 37' 23" S
13° 28' 34" E

D3702

Kunene River Lodge

Ehomba

STEILRAND MTS

D3700

D3720

17° 51' 45" S
13° 01' 26" E

tanga

Otjivero

D3703

18° 03' 29" S
13° 15' 31" E

GIRAFFEN MTS

Hoarusib

Otjiu

Spring

D3707

Dorsland Trek Church Ruin

Opuwo

Oruwanje

D3705

Kaoko Otavi

C43

D3710

D3709

D

ANGOLA

View of Waterfall

17° 24' 46" S
14° 21' 19" E

Ruacana Falls

Ruacana

D3617

State Forest

C35

80

C41

18° 08' 39" S
14° 17' 26" E

C35

Otjitoko

Kaokoland

JOUBERTBERGE

Okatumba

Robbie's Pass

Otjikondavirongo

D3705

D3707

Tomakas

Ganamub

Ganamub

19° 07' 32" S
13° 37' 01" E

Sesfontein

Old Fort

Fort Sesfontein

Otjitaimo

C43

Otjomatemba

18° 41' 45" S
14° 15' 26" E

D3708

Ombombo

Dorslandtrekkers Monument

Otjitunduwa Otjondeka

Okatjiura

18° 43' 15" S
13° 55' 19" E

D3710

C43

Blinkwater Falls

Warmquelle

D3708

Kowares

C35

Aasvoëlbad

Hoanib

Dubis

Kunene

72

Khowarib

Khowarib

Baadjie

79

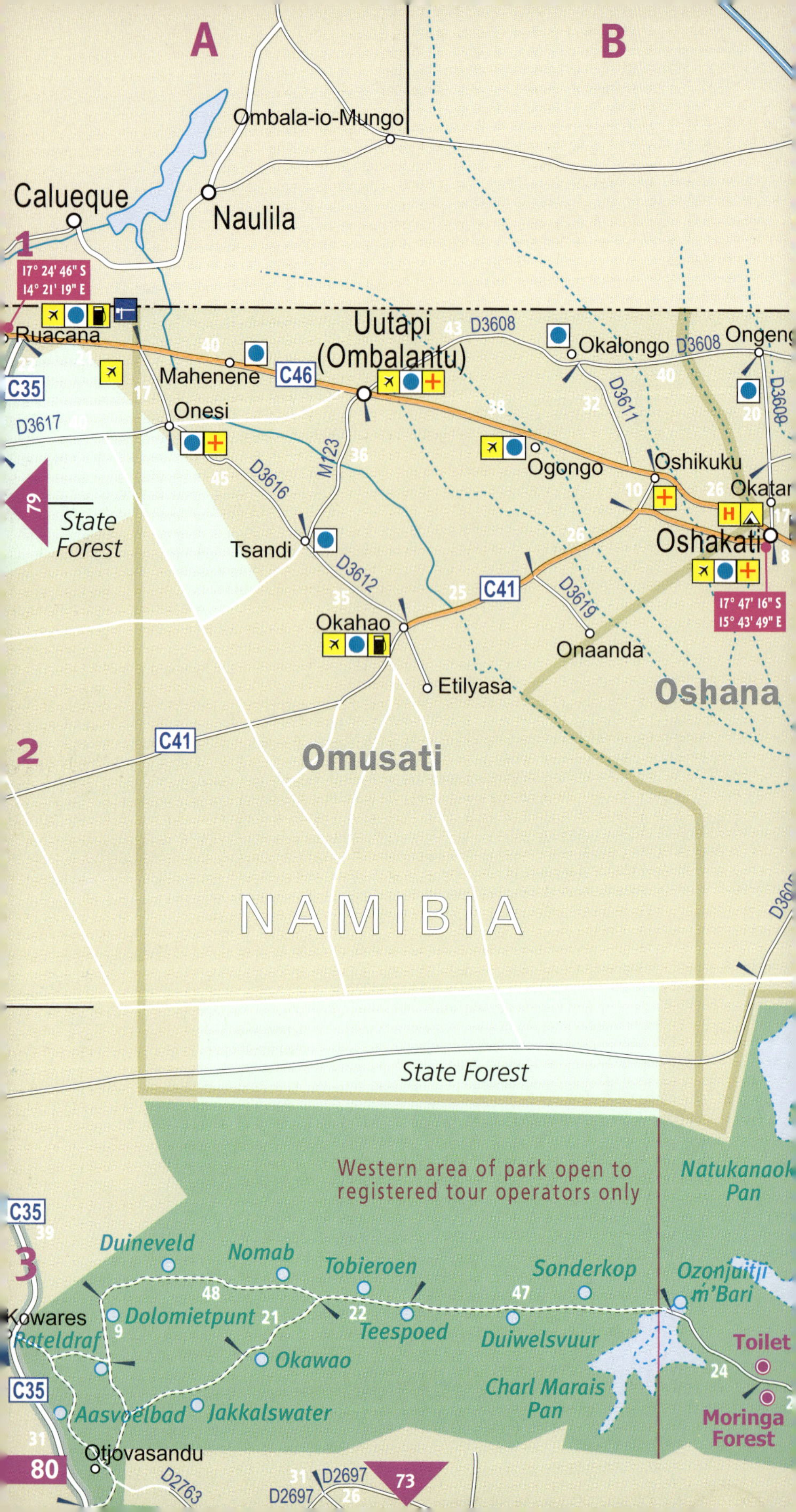
A
B
1
2
3
Ombala-io-Mungo
Calueque
Naulila
17° 24' 46" S
14° 21' 19" E
Ruacana
Mahenene
C46
Uutapi
(Ombalantu)
D3608
Okalongo
Ongeng
C35
D3617
Onesi
M123
D3616
D3611
D3609
Ogongo
Oshikuku
Okatar
Oshakati
17° 47' 16" S
15° 43' 49" E
79
State
Forest
Tsandi
D3612
C41
D3619
Okahao
Onaanda
Etilyasa
Oshana
Omusati
NAMIBIA
State Forest
Western area of park open to
registered tour operators only
Natukanaok
Pan
Duineveld
Nomab
Tobieroen
Sonderkop
Ozonjuitji
m'Bari
Kowares
Dolomietpunt
Teespoed
Duiwelsvuur
Toilet
Rateldraf
Okawao
Charl Marais
Pan
Moringa
Forest
Aasvoëlbad
Jakkalswater
Otjovasandu
80
D2763
D2697
73

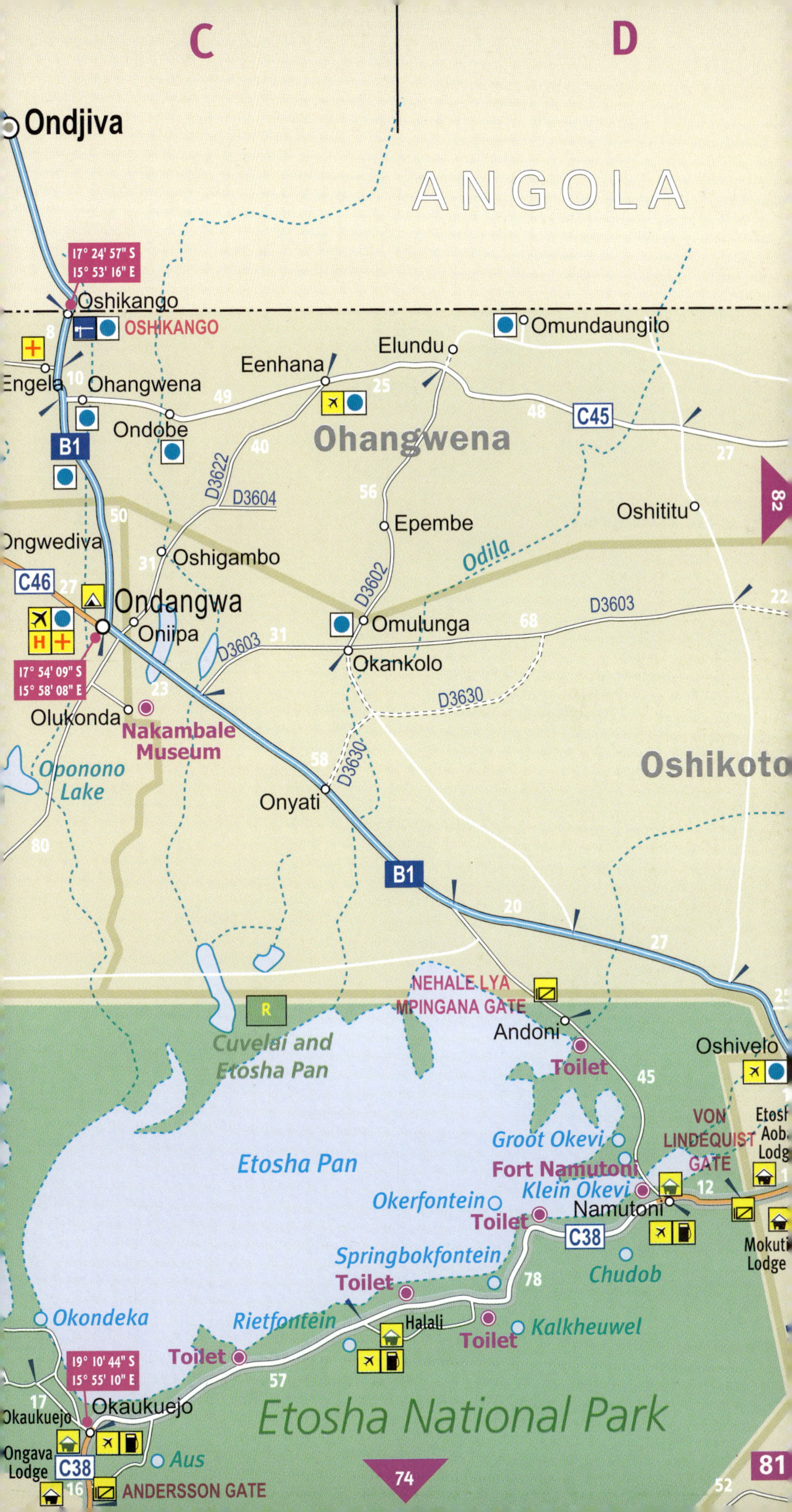
C
D
Ondjiva
ANGOLA
17° 24' 57" S
15° 53' 16" E
Oshikango
OSHIKANGO
Omundaungilo
Elundu
Eenhana
Engela
Ohangwena
Ondobe
C45
B1
Ohangwena
D3622
D3604
Epembe
Oshititu
82
Ongwediva
Oshigambo
Odila
C46
Ondangwa
Oniipa
D3602
Omulunga
D3603
D3603
Okankolo
17° 54' 09" S
15° 58' 08" E
D3630
Olukonda
Nakambale
Museum
Oshikoto
Oponono
Lake
Onyati
D3630
B1
NEHALE LYA
MPINGANA GATE
Andoni
R
Cuvelai and
Etosha Pan
Toilet
Oshivelo
Etosha Pan
Groot Okevi
VON
LINDEQUIST
GATE
Fort Namutoni
Klein Okevi
Okerfontein
Namutoni
Toilet
C38
Mokuti
Lodge
Springbokfontein
Chudob
Toilet
Okondeka
Rietfontein
Halali
Toilet
Kalkheuwel
Toilet
19° 10' 44" S
15° 55' 10" E
Okaukuejo
Okaukuejo
Etosha National Park
Ongava
Lodge
C38
Aus
ANDERSSON GATE
74
81

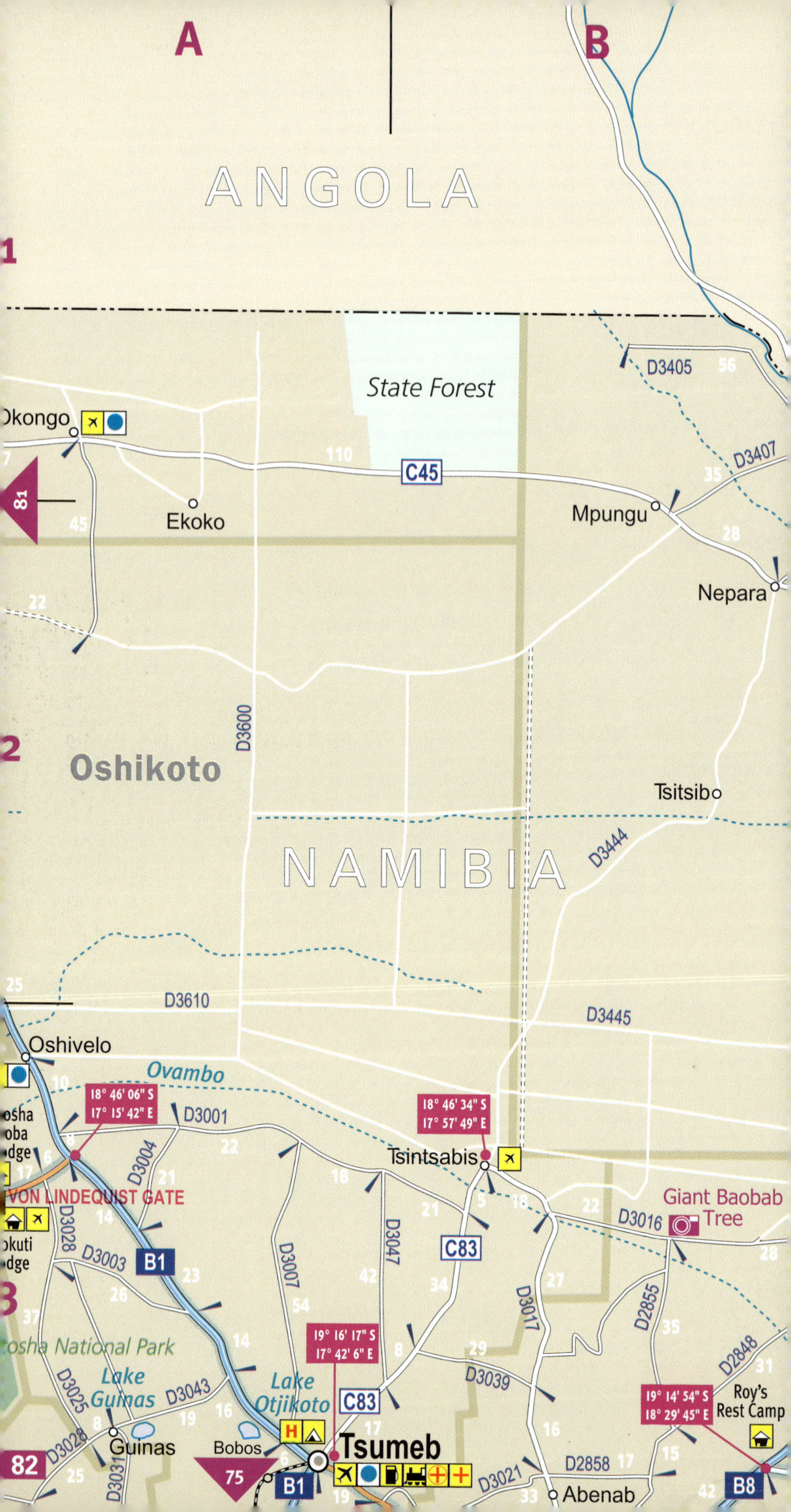
A
B
1
2
3
ANGOLA
State Forest
Okongo
C45
110
Ekoko
81
45
22
Mpungu
Nepara
28
35
D3405
56
D3407
D3600
Oshikoto
Tsitsibo
NAMIBIA
D3444
25
D3610
D3445
Oshivelo
Ovambo
18° 46' 06" S
17° 15' 42" E
D3001
D3004
18° 46' 34" S
17° 57' 49" E
Tsintsabis
VON LINDEQUIST GATE
Giant Baobab Tree
D3016
C83
D3028
D3003
B1
D3007
D3047
D3017
D2855
D2848
osha National Park
Lake Guinas
D3043
Lake Otjikoto
19° 16' 17" S
17° 42' 6" E
D3039
19° 14' 54" S
18° 29' 45" E
Roy's Rest Camp
D3025
Guinas
Bobos
Tsumeb
75
D3028
D3031
D3021
D2858
Abenab
B8
82

C

D

Luena National Park

Cuito

Kavango

Cuangar
Nkurenkuru
Maiuvo
Tondoro
Rupara
Calai
Sambusu
Kavango River Lodge
Ngandu Safari Lodge
Hakusemba Lodge
Mutanc
Rundu
Nkwazi Lodge
Kaiso Lodg

C45
D3406
D3405
C45
B8
D3425

17° 56' 19" S
19° 45' 13" E

84

Kavango

Khaudum

B8

Ncaute

150

Mangetti
Mururani
D3016
D2908
D2848
D3016
Maanlig
D2898
D3425

Karakuwisa

Omatako
D3308

Maroelaboom
D2845
Kano Vlei
C44

76

83

A
B

1

Mutango
Utokota 50 Mashari 20 Dirico
B8
D3400
Nyangana 56
B8 81
D3309
83
Taratara
D3403

Kavango

D3400

18° 35' 39" S
20° 33' 45" E

Tamsu Khaudum

Doringstraat Waterhole

2

Khaudum Game Park

Elands Drink Waterhole

Dussi Waterhole

Nhoma

Sikereti *Soncana Waterhole*

Samagaigai

Nhoma
Nhoma D3303 D3311 D3303 D3315 D3303
D3312

Dorsland Trek Baobab

Aasvoëlnes Klein Dobe

3

C44 27
D3301 29 14
19° 35' 35" S
20° 30' 22" E
DOBE
14 Quankwa
Tsumkwe Lodge Holboom Makuri M74 31 35
Otjozondjupa Tsumkwe
Holboom Djokwe **Grootboom (Giant Baobab Tree)**
84 37 D3302 42 77 C44
Tweeputte Caecae (Xaixai)

C | D

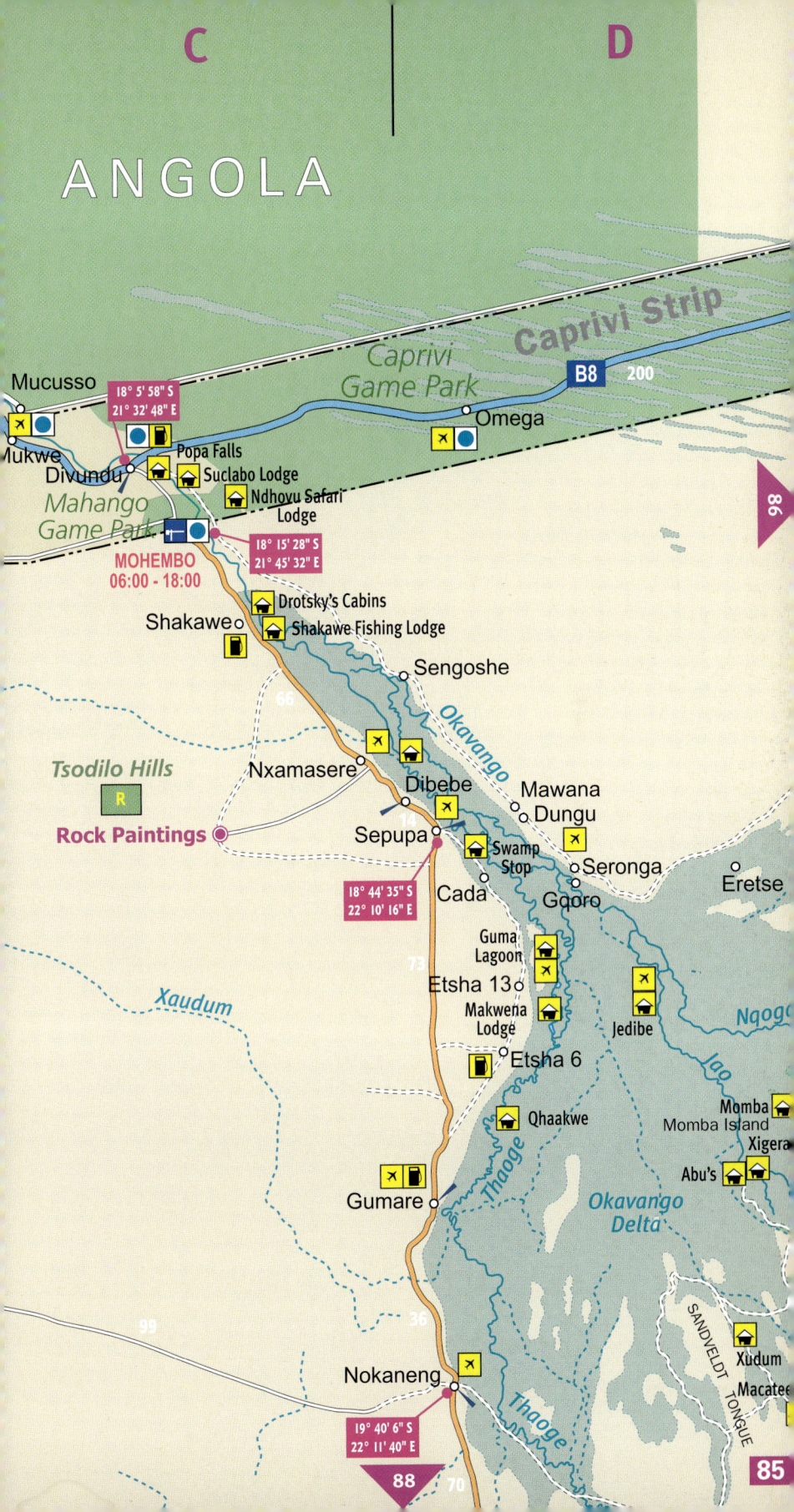

ANGOLA

Caprivi Strip

Caprivi Game Park

B8 200

Mucusso

18° 5' 58" S
21° 32' 48" E

Mukwe
Divundu
Popa Falls
Suclabo Lodge
Ndhovu Safari Lodge

Omega

Mahango Game Park

MOHEMBO
06:00 - 18:00

18° 15' 28" S
21° 45' 32" E

Drotsky's Cabins
Shakawe
Shakawe Fishing Lodge

Sengoshe

Okavango

Tsodilo Hills
R
Rock Paintings

Nxamasere
Dibebe
Mawana
Dungu

Sepupa
Swamp Stop
Seronga
Eretse

18° 44' 35" S
22° 10' 16" E

Cada
Gqoro

Guma Lagoon
Etsha 13
Makwena Lodge
Jedibe

Xaudum

Etsha 6

Ngogo

Qhaakwe
Momba
Momba Island
Xigera
Abu's

Gumare

Thaoge

Okavango Delta

SANDVELDT TONGUE

Xudum
Macatee

Nokaneng

19° 40' 6" S
22° 11' 40" E

Thaoge

A
B
Sioma Ngwezi National Park
Luiana
ANGOLA
17° 47' 9" S
23° 22' 42" E
State Forest
B8
1
Caprivi Strip
Kongola
Sibinda
Kubunyana
Susuwe Island Lodge
Nambwa
Namushasha Lodge
NAMIBIA
Mudumu National Park
D3501
Lizauli Traditional Village
Lianshulu
Linyandi
Linyandi
85
Lagoon
Kwando
Sangwali
Shaile
Game Scout Camp
Linyandi Swamp
Linyandi
Mamili National Park
King's Pool
Duma Tau
Lloyd's
Savuti
Selinda
Zibadianja
Savuti
Savuti South
Zibadianja Pan
Alan's
Game Scout Camp
Savuti Marsh
2
Magwegqana
Betsaa
Motswiri
MAGWIKHWE SAND RIDGE
Mababe Depression
Xugana Lodge
MABABE GATE
Xugana
Kwara
Shindi Lodge
Okavango
KHWAI GATE (North Gate)
Xakanaxa
Moremi
Okuti
Xobega
Mboroga
Third Bridge
Moremi Game Reserve
Guekha
Chief's Island
MAQWEE GATE (South Gate)
Gomoti
946m
3
Chitabe
San-ta-Wani Lodge
Delta
Xaxaba
Gunn's
Oddball's
Santantadibe
Drift
Pom Pom
Semetsi
Lion's Island
Bokwi Island
Bobo Island
Macateer's
Beacon Island
Boro
Shorobe
KHURUNXARAGA GATE
89
Crocodile Camp

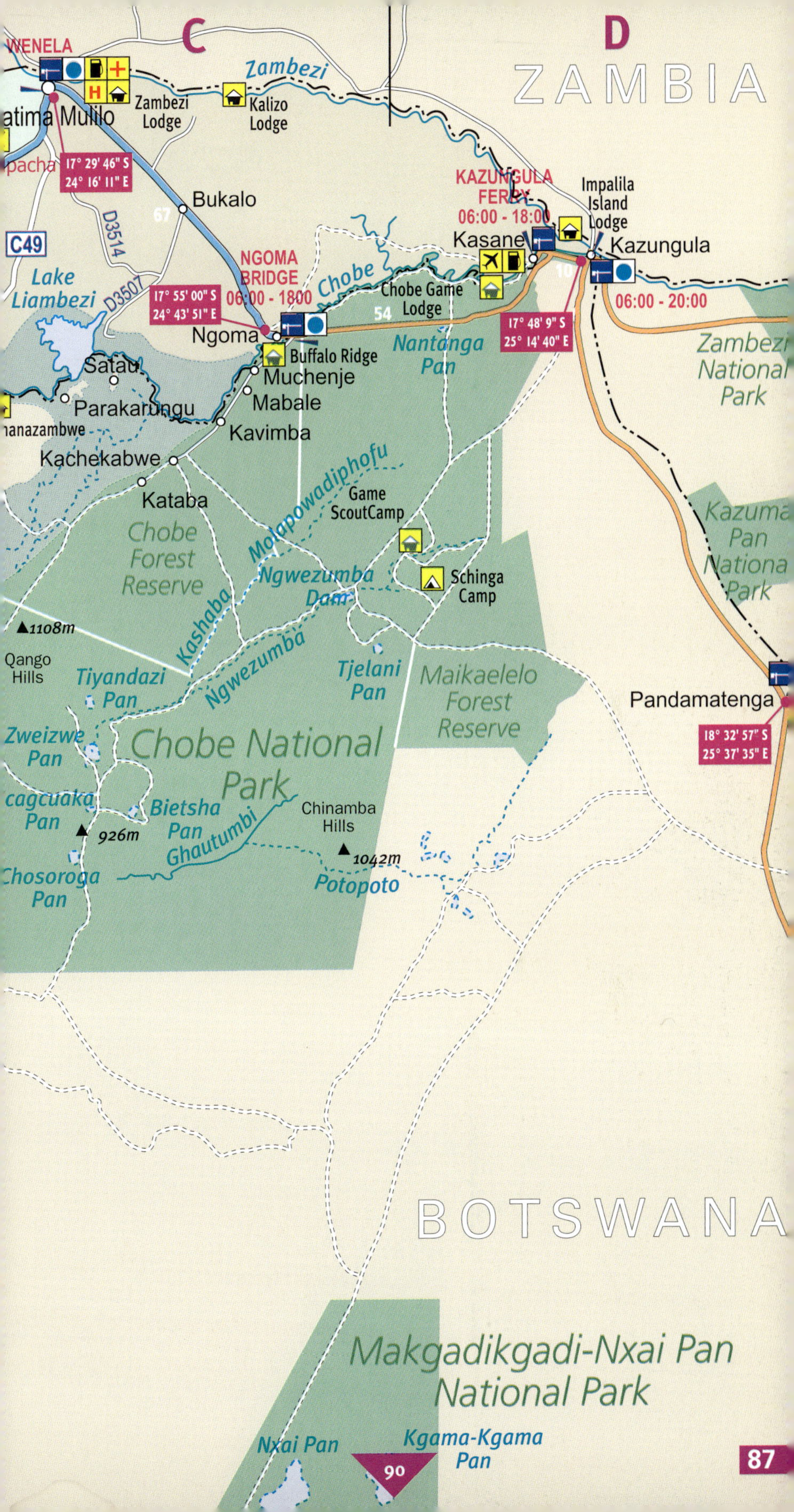

C
D
ZAMBIA
WENELA
Zambezi
atima Mulilo
Zambezi Lodge
Kalizo Lodge
pacha
17° 29' 46" S
24° 16' 11" E
Bukalo
67
C49
D3514
Lake Liambezi
D3507
NGOMA BRIDGE
06:00 - 1800
17° 55' 00" S
24° 43' 51" E
Chobe
Ngoma
Buffalo Ridge
Chobe Game Lodge
54
KAZUNGULA FERRY
06:00 - 18:00
Kasane
Impalila Island Lodge
Kazungula
10
06:00 - 20:00
17° 48' 9" S
25° 14' 40" E
Nantanga Pan
Zambezi National Park
Satau
Muchenje
Mabale
Parakarungu
Kavimba
anazambwe
Kachekabwe
Kataba
Molapowadiphofu
Game ScoutCamp
Kazuma Pan National Park
Chobe Forest Reserve
Ngwezumba Dam
Schinga Camp
1108m
Kashaba
Qango Hills
Tiyandazi Pan
Ngwezumba
Tjelani Pan
Maikaelelo Forest Reserve
Pandamatenga
18° 32' 57" S
25° 37' 35" E
Zweizwe Pan
Chobe National Park
cagcuaka Pan
Bietsha Pan
Chinamba Hills
926m
Ghautumbi
1042m
Chosoroga Pan
Potopoto
BOTSWANA
Makgadikgadi-Nxai Pan National Park
Nxai Pan
Kgama-Kgama Pan
90

A

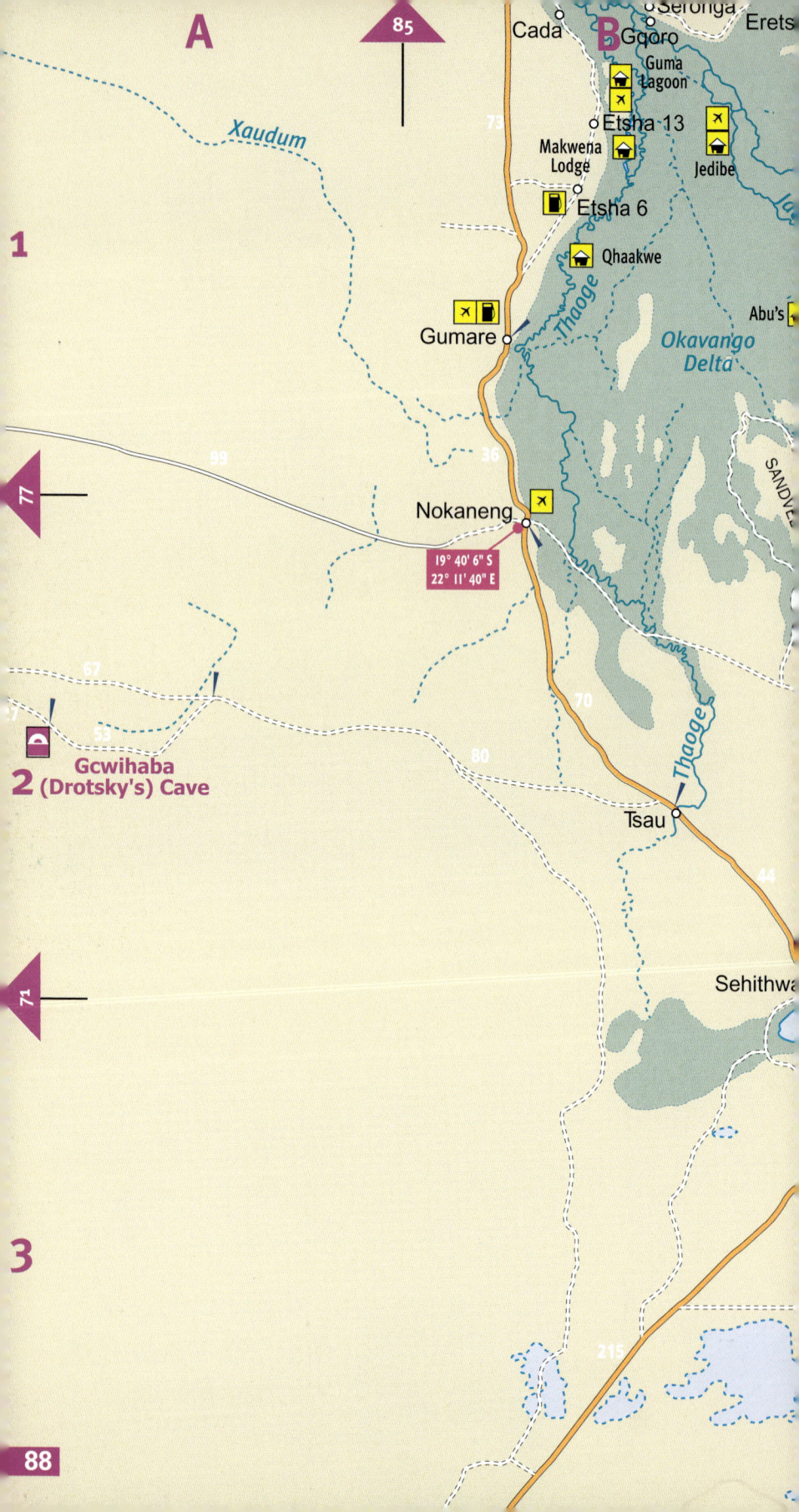

B

1

Xaudum

85

Cada
Seronga
Gqoro
Guma Lagoon
Etsha 13
Makwena Lodge
Jedibe
Etsha 6
Qhaakwe
Thaoge
Abu's
Okavango Delta
Gumare

77

Nokaneng
19° 40' 6" S
22° 11' 40" E

SANDV

2

Gcwihaba (Drotsky's) Cave

Thaoge
Tsau

71

Sehithwa

3

88

Map: Okavango Delta / Moremi Game Reserve area, Botswana

C — Motswiri

86

D — MAGWIKHWE SAND RIDGE, MABABE GATE

Okavango Delta lodges and camps

- Xugana Lodge
- Xugana
- Kwara
- Shindi Lodge
- Okavango
- Xakanaxa
- Moremi
- Okuti
- Third Bridge
- Xobega
- Mboroga
- Momba
- Momba Island
- Xigera
- Chief's Island
- Guekha
- Gomoti
- **Moremi Game Reserve**
- **KHWAI GATE (North Gate)** — 19° 10' 25" S, 23° 45' 5" E
- **MAQWEE GATE (South Gate)**
- San-ta-Wani Lodge
- 946m
- Delta
- Xaxaba
- Gunn's
- Oddball's
- Chitabe
- Semetsi
- Lion's Island
- Bokwi Island
- Bobo Island
- Pom Pom
- Macateer's
- Beacon Island
- Santantadibe
- Boro
- Drift
- Shorobe
- 27
- 37
- **KHURUNXARAGA GATE**
- Island Safari Lodge
- Crocodile Camp
- Okavango River Lodge
- Audi Camp
- **Old Bridge**
- **Maun** — 19° 59' 57" S, 23° 24' 54" E
- **MATSIBI GATE**
- 59
- 28
- Boteti
- 14
- Makalamabedi
- 71
- Nhabe
- Toteng — 20° 21' 34" S, 22° 57' 34" E
- 32
- Lake Ngami

BOTSWANA

90

Central Kalahari Game Reserve

89

Makgadikgadi-Nxai Pan National Park

BOTSWANA

Labels on map

- Chosoroga Pan
- Potopoto
- North Camp (Only open to HATAB members)
- Nxai Pan
- Kgama-Kgama Pan
- South Camp
- Game Scout Camp
- 956m
- Bushman Pits
- Kanyu
- Phuduhudu
- Kudiakam Pan
- Baines' Baobabs
- Game Scout Camp
- Gweta
- 20° 11' 42" S
- 25° 15' 28" E
- Planet Baobab
- Motopi Ford
- Moremaoto
- 20° 13' 10" S
- 24° 9' 11" E
- Gweta Lodge
- Khumaga
- Green's Baobab
- Khumaga
- Game Scout Camp
- Njuca Hills
- Chapman's Baobab
- Tsoe
- Ntwetwe Pan
- Sukwane
- Rakops
- 21° 0' 57" S
- 24° 21' 42" E
- Dzibui Pan
- Guguago Pan
- Nkokwane Pan
- View of Sua Pan
- Xhumo
- Boteti
- Mopipi
- Lake Xau
- Mopipi Dam
- Tsokotsa Pan
- Rysana Pan
- Mmatshum

Index

NAME	GRID	PG	NAME	GRID	PG	NAME	GRID	PG
Aasvoëlnes	A3	84	Divundu	C1	85	Goageb	D3	59
Aasvoëlnes	C2	77	Djokwe	A3	84	Gobabeb	B2	62
Abenab	B3	82	Djokwe	C2	77	Gobabis	A3	70
Abenab	D2	75	Dordabis	A1	64	Gochas	C1	61
Ai-Ais	A2	56	Doreenville	B1	64	Gochas	C3	65
Akanous	D1	61	Doreenville	D3	69	Goodhouse	B3	56
Akanous	D1	65	Doros	C1	67	Goreis	A3	74
Alexander Bay	C3	55	Drimiopsis	A3	70	Gqoro	B1	88
Ameib	D2	67	Du Plessis	B2	70	Gqoro	D2	85
Aminuis	D1	65	Dubis	A2	72	Grootberg	C2	73
Amspoort	A2	72	Dubis	C3	79	Grootfontein	D1	59
Andoni	B1	74	Duineveld	A2	64	Grootfontein	D2	75
Andoni	D3	81	Dungu	D2	85	Gross Ums	C1	65
Arandis	D3	67	Eenhana	C1	81	Grünau	B2	56
Aranos	C3	65	Ehomba	D1	79	Guinas	A3	82
Ariamsvlei	D2	57	Eindpaal	C2	61	Guinas	C2	75
Aris	B3	68	Eirup	B3	64	Gumare	B1	88
Aris	D1	63	Ekoko	A2	82	Gumare	D3	85
Aroab	D1	57	Eksteenfontein	A3	56	Gunab	A3	60
Aroab	D3	61	Eksteenfontein	D3	55	Gweta	B2	90
Asab	B2	60	Elunda	D1	81	Hanaus	A2	60
Aukam	D1	55	Engela	C1	81	Haribes	A1	60
Aus	C1	55	Enyandi	C1	79	Haribes	A3	64
Aus	C3	59	Epembe	C1	79	Haris	B3	68
Aussenkehr	A3	56	Epembe	C2	81	Haris	D1	63
Baadjie	B2	72	Epukiro	B2	70	Hartseer	B3	74
Baadjie	D3	79	Epupa	D1	67	Haruchas	C3	63
Bergsig	B3	72	Epupa	D3	73	Hebron	C1	69
Berseba	A2	60	Eremutua	A1	68	Helena	C2	71
Bethanie	A3	60	Eretse	B1	88	Helmeringhausen	D2	59
Bethanie	D3	59	Eretse	D2	85	Henties Bay	C3	67
Betsaa	A2	86	Erundu	B1	68	Heuningberg	B3	74
Biermanskool	D2	73	Erundu	B3	74	Hoaseb	C1	65
Bladgrond	D3	57	Esere	C3	75	Hochveld	C2	69
Brack	A1	64	Etanga	C2	79	Hohental	C2	75
Brack	C3	69	Etemba	A2	68	Homeb	B2	62
Brandberg West	B1	66	Etemba	D2	67	Hottentot's Bay	A3	58
Brukkaros	B2	60	Etengwa	B1	78	Huns	D2	59
Buitepos	C3	71	Etilyasa	B2	80	Huns	A1	56
Bukalo	C1	87	Etjo	B1	68	Huns	D1	55
Bulwana	B1	60	Etsha 6	B1	88	Inachab	A1	56
Bushman Pits	A2	90	Etsha 6	D3	85	Kachekabwe	C1	87
Cada	B1	88	Etsha	B1	88	Kakus	A3	70
Cada	D2	85	Etsha	D2	85	Kakus	C1	65
Caecae (Xaixai)	B3	84	Evero	B2	68	Kalkrand	A2	64
Caecae (Xaixai)	C2	77	Fransfontein	D3	73	Kalkveld	A1	68
Calai	D2	83	Gagarus	D2	73	Kamanjab	C2	73
Calueque	A1	80	Gainatseb	D3	73	Kano Vlei	B2	76
Cauas	D3	73	Gam	D3	77	Kano Vlei	D3	83
Chaibis	C1	63	Ganab	B1	62	Kanyu	A2	90
Coblenz	D3	75	Ganamub	A1	72	Kaoko Otavi	B1	72
Cuangar	C1	83	Ganamub	C3	79	Kaoko Otavi	C2	79
Dabenoris	B3	56	Garib	A1	64	Kapp's Farm	A1	64
Derm	B2	64	Garinais	C3	61	Kapp's Farm	C3	69
Dibebe	D2	85	Gibeon	A1	60	Karakuwisa	B1	76
Dirico	B1	84	Girib	A2	64	Karakuwisa	D3	83
Dis Al	A2	70	Goageb	D1	55	Karasburg	B2	56

91

Index Index Index Index Index

NAME	GRID	PG	NAME	GRID	PG	NAME	GRID	PG
Karibib	A2	68	Mooifontein	D2	59	Okandjombo	B2	78
Kasane	D1	87	Mopipi	A3	90	Okangwati	C1	79
Kataba	C1	87	Moremaoto	A2	90	Okankolo	C2	81
Katima Mulilo	C1	87	Motopi	A2	90	Okarukurume	A2	70
Kavimba	C1	87	Motsomi	D1	65	Okarukurume	D2	69
Kazungula	D1	87	Mpungu	B2	82	Okasewa	B1	64
Keetmanshoop	B3	60	Muchenje	C1	87	Okasewa	D3	69
Keitsas	A3	70	Mucusso	C1	85	Okatana	B1	80
Keitsas	C1	65	Mukwe	C1	85	Okatjiura	B1	72
Khaudum	B2	84	Mururani	A1	76	Okatjiura	D3	79
Khaudum	D1	77	Mururani	C3	83	Okatumba	B1	72
Khorixas	C3	73	Mutango	A1	84	Okatumba	C3	79
Khowarib	B2	72	Mutango	D2	83	Okatuwo	B2	70
Khowarib	D3	79	Nabies	D3	57	Okaukuejo	A1	74
Khubus	D3	55	Nama Pan	D3	77	Okaukuejo	C3	81
Khumaga	A3	90	Namutoni	B1	74	Okauwe	B1	78
Klein Aub	D2	63	Namutoni	D3	81	Okavarumendu	A2	70
Klein Dobe	A3	84	Nanzes	B2	56	Okave	B3	74
Klein Dobe	C2	77	Naos	D1	63	Okombahe	D2	67
Klein Nauas	B2	64	Narubis	B1	56	Okondjatu	D1	69
Klein-Karas	B2	56	Nauchas	C2	63	Okongo	A1	82
Koës	C2	61	Naulila	A1	80	Okovimburu	B2	70
Kokerboom	C2	57	Nauzerus	C2	63	Okozondara	A2	70
Kolmanskop	B1	54	Ncaute	C1	77	Olukonda	C2	81
Kolmanskop	B3	58	Ncaute	D2	83	Omahoro	D1	67
Komukanti	C2	75	Neina	B3	74	Omaruru	A2	68
Kongola	A1	86	Neineis	D2	67	Omatako	B2	68
Kowares	A3	80	Neisip	D3	59	Omatjete	D1	67
Kowares	C1	73	Nepara	B2	82	Ombala-io-Mungo	A1	80
Kowares	D3	79	Neuras	C1	59	Ombombo	B1	72
Lekkersing	D3	55	Neuras	C3	63	Ombombo	D3	79
Leonardville	C2	65	Ngoma	C1	87	Omega	D1	85
Lidfontein	B3	64	Nhoma	A3	84	Omitara	D3	69
Linyandi	B1	86	Nhoma	B2	84	Omulunga	C2	81
Lüderitz	B1	54	Nhoma	C2	77	Omundaungilo	D1	81
Lüderitz	B3	58	Nhoma	D1	77	Onaanda	B2	80
Luhebu	B2	76	Nina	B1	64	Ondangwa	C2	81
Luiana	A1	86	Nkurenkuru	C1	83	Onderombapa	D1	65
Maanlig	A2	76	Noenieput	D2	57	Ondjiva	C1	81
Maanlig	C3	83	Nokaneng	B2	88	Ondobe	C1	81
Mabale	C1	87	Nokaneng	D3	85	Onesi	A1	80
Mahenene	A1	80	Nomtsas	D3	63	Ongenga	B1	80
Maiuvo	C2	83	Noordoewer	A3	56	Ongwediva	B2	80
Makalamabedi	D2	89	Nugubaes	A3	74	Oniipa	C2	81
Maltahöhe	D1	59	Nxamasere	C2	85	Onseepkans	C3	57
Maltahöhe	D3	63	Nyanganga	B1	84	Onyati	C2	81
Mangetti	A1	76	Obobogorab	D1	57	Opuwo	D2	77
Mangetti	C3	83	Ogongo	B1	80	Oranjemund	C3	55
Mariental	B1	60	Ohangwena	C1	81	Orupembe	B2	78
Mariental	B3	64	Okahandja	B2	68	Orusewa	D1	67
Maroelaboom	A2	76	Okahao	A2	80	Orusewa	D3	73
Maroelaboom	C3	83	Okakarara	C1	69	Oruwanje	A1	72
Mashari	A1	84	Okakarara	C3	75	Oruwanje	C2	79
Maun	C2	89	Okalongo	B1	80	Osamba	D3	69
Mawana	D2	85	Okamatapati	D1	69	Oshakati	B2	80
Mmatshumo	A3	90	Okamatapati	D3	75	Oshigambo	C2	81
Mon Desir	D2	73	Okandjombo	A1	72	Oshikango	C1	81

Index

NAME	GRID	PG	NAME	GRID	PG	NAME	GRID	PG
Oshikuku	B1	80	Quankwa	D2	77	Tomakas	C3	79
Oshititu	D2	81	Rakops	A3	90	Tondoro	C2	83
Oshivelo	A3	82	Rehoboth	D2	63	Torra Bay	A3	72
Oshivelo	C1	75	Rietfontein	D1	57	Toteng	C2	89
Oshivelo	D3	81	Rietfontein	D2	71	Tsandi	A2	80
Osire	C1	69	Rietfontein	D2	75	Tsaraxaibis	C2	57
Otavi	C2	75	Rietfontein	D3	61	Tsau	B2	88
Otjahevita	C3	75	Rietoog	D2	63	Tses	B2	60
Otjenga	B3	74	Rooibank	A1	62	Tsintsabis	B3	82
Otjihorongo	D1	67	Rosh Pinah	D2	55	Tsintsabis	D1	75
Otjikango	B3	74	Ruacana	A1	80	Tsitsib	B2	82
Otjikondavirongo	A2	71	Ruacana	D1	79	Tsoe	A3	90
Otjikondavirongo	C3	79	Rundu	D2	83	Tsootsha	D3	71
Otjiveze	C1	79	Rupara	C2	83	Tsumeb	A3	82
Otjikondo	D2	73	Samagaigai	A3	84	Tsumeb	C2	75
Otjimbingwe	A3	68	Samagaigai	C2	77	Tsumkwe	A3	84
Otjimbovo	A2	68	Sambusu	D2	83	Tsumkwe	C2	77
Otjimukandi	A3	70	Sangwali	B2	86	Tubusis	D2	67
Otjinene	A1	70	Sanitatas	B2	78	Tutara	D3	73
Otjinoko	B2	70	Satau	C1	87	Twee Rivier	C2	61
Otjinungwa	B1	78	Savuti	B2	86	Tweeputte	C3	77
Otjisemba	B2	68	Schlip	A2	64	Uhlenhorst	B2	64
Otjitambi	D2	73	Schlip	D2	63	Uis	C2	67
Otjitanda	B1	78	Seeheim	A1	56	Union's End	D1	61
Otjitasu	A1	68	Seeheim	A3	60	Union's End	D1	65
Otjitasu	A3	74	Sehithwa	B2	88	Usakos	D2	67
Otjitoko	B1	72	Sendelingsdrif	D2	55	Us	C1	63
Otjitoko	D2	79	Sengoshe	D2	85	Utokota	A1	84
Otjitunduwa	B1	72	Sepupa	D2	85	Uutapi(Ombalantu)	A1	80
Otjituuo	A2	76	Seronga	B1	88	Velloorsdrif	C3	57
Otjiu	C2	79	Seronga	D2	85	Vioolsdrif	A3	56
Otjiwarongo	B1	68	Sesfontein	B2	72	Vogelweide	C2	65
Otjiwarongo	B3	74	Sesfontein	C3	79	Vredeshoop	C1	57
Otjiyarwa	B2	70	Shakawe	C2	85	Vrindskap	A3	74
Otjomatemba	B1	72	Shorobe	B3	86	Walvis Bay	A1	62
Otjomatemba	D3	79	Shorobe	D2	89	Warmbad	B3	56
Otjondeka	B1	72	Sibinda	B1	86	Warmfontein	C1	57
Otjondeka	D3	79	Sikereti	B3	84	Warmquelle	B2	72
Otjosondu	D2	69	Sikereti	D2	77	Warmquelle	D3	79
Otjovasandu	A3	80	Solitaire	C2	63	Wegdraai	C2	61
Otjovasandu	C2	73	Sorris Sorris	C1	67	Weissbrünn	C2	73
Otjumue	A2	68	Stampriet	B3	64	Welverdiend	D2	61
Otjumue	D2	67	Steinhausen	D2	69	Wereldsend	B3	72
Outjo	A3	74	Sukses	B1	68	Wilhelmstal	A2	68
Ozondati	D1	67	Sukwane	A3	90	Windhoek	B3	68
Ozondjache	B1	68	Summerdown	A2	70	Windhoek	D1	63
Ozondjache	B3	74	Summerdown	D2	69	Witbooisvlei	B1	60
Palmwag	B3	72	Swakopmund	A1	62	Witpütz	D2	55
Pandamatenga	D2	87	Swakopmund	C3	67	Witvlei	A3	70
Parakarungu	C1	87	Swartbooisdrift	D1	79	Wlotzkas Baken	C3	67
Pella	C3	57	Talismanis	D2	71	Xanagas	C3	71
Persip	C2	61	Tamsu	A2	84	Xhumo	A3	90
Phuduhudu	A2	90	Tamsu	D1	77	Zaris	C1	59
Pomona	B1	54	Taratara	A1	84			
Purros	A1	72	Terrace Bay	A3	72			
Purros	B3	78	Tjirundo	A2	68			
Quankwa	B3	84	Tomakas	A1	72			

93

Resources Resources Resources

NAMIBIAN CONTACT DETAILS & INFORMATION

Namibia (country code 00264)

Namibian Tourism Board
Tel: 61 290 6000
Fax: 61 254 848/401
www.namibiatourism.com.na

Namibia Wildlife Resorts & Reservations
Tel: 61 285 7000/7200
Fax: 61 224 900
www.nwr.com.na

Namibia Wildlife Resorts
Tel: 61 23 6975/6/7/8
Fax: 61 22 4 900

Police
The national emergency number for the Police is 10111.

Telephone enquiries
For numbers that have changed or are not listed in the telephone directory, dial 1188.

Gobabis (062)
Municipality
Tel: 56 2551
Fax: 56 3012/2428

Uaki Wilderness Tourist Info
Tel: 56 4743
Fax: 56 4169

Ministry of Environment and Tourism
Tel: 56 2428
Fax: 56 3028

Municipality
Tel: 56 2551/4847/4842
Fax: 56 3012/2428

Grootfontein (067)
Tourist info
Tel: 24 3100/1/4

Municipal & Tourism Office
Tel: 24 3101/100/109
Fax: 24 2930
www.grootfonteinmun.com.na

Henties Bay (064)
Tourist office
Tel: 50 1143
Fax: 50 1142
www.hentiesbaytourism.com

Municipality
Tel: 50 2000
Fax: 50 2001

Katima Mulilo (066)
Tourist office
Tutwa Tourism and Travel
Tel/Fax: 25 2739/3048
www.tutwa.com

Municipality
Tel: 25 3586/3003
Fax: 25 3212

Keetmanshoop (063)
Ministry of Environment & Tourism
Tel: 22 3223
Fax: 22 5629

Southern Tourist Forum
Tel: 22 1266/11
Fax: 22 3813/8

Municipality
Tel: 22 1212/11
Fax: 22 3818

Lüderitz (063)
Tourist office
Tel: 20 2719/20 2622
Fax: 20 4188/2863

Lüderitz Town Council
Tel: 20 2041
Fax: 20 2971

Mariental (063)
Ministry of Environment & Tourism
Tel: 24 2427
Fax: 24 0885

Municipality
Tel: 24 0347/5600
Fax: 24 2039

Okahandja (062)
Gross Barmen Hot Springs Resort
Tel: 50 1091
Fax: 50 1094

Municipality
Tel: 50 5100
Fax: 50 1746

Omaruru (064)
Ministry of Environment and Tourism - Tourist Info
Tel: 57 1194
Fax: 57 1195

Municipality
Tel: 57 0028
Fax: 57 0105

Opuwo (065)
Ministry of Environment & Tourism
Tel: 27 3003
Fax: 27 3171/27 3152

The Kaoko Info Centre
Tel: 27 3420

Municipality
Tel: 27 3007/3070
Fax: 27 3250/65

Oshakati (065)
Municipality
Tel: 22 9500
Fax: 22 0435

Otavi (067)
Municipality & Village Council
Tel: 23 4022
Fax: 23 4236

Otjiwarongo (067)
Tourist office/Omaue Information
Tel/Fax: 30 3830/30 2231

Municipality
Tel: 30 2231
Fax: 30 2098

Outjo (067)
Etosha Information Bureau
Tel/Fax: 31 3072

Municipality
Tel: 31 3013/113
Fax: 31 3065

Rehoboth (062)
Town Council of Rehoboth
Tel: 52 1800
Fax: 52 2090/92

Rundu (066)
Ministry of Environment & Tourism
Tel: 25 5749
Fax: 25 5789
www.met.gov.na

Rundu Tourist Info
Tel: 25 6140

Municipality/Town Council
Tel: 26 6400
Fax: 25 6718/787

Resources

TOURIST INFORMATION

Sesfontein (065)
Fort Sesfontein Lodge
Tel: 68 5034
Fax: 68 5033
www.fort-sesfontein.com.na

Swakopmund (064)
Namib-i
Tel: 40 4827
Fax: 40 3129
www.namibi.org.na

Municipality
Tel: 410 4111
Fax: 410 4208
www.swkmun.com.na

Tsumeb (067)
Tourist office
Travel North Namibia
Tel: 22 0728
Fax: 22 0916
www.natron.net/tnn

Municipality
Tel: 22 1056
Fax: 22 1467/4

Walvis Bay (064)
Tourist office
Tel: 20 9170
Fax: 20 9171
www.walvisbay.com.na

Municipality
Tel: 201 3111
Fax: 20 4528

Windhoek (061)
Information Office
Tel: 290 2092/2401/2596
Fax: 290 2203
www.windhoekcc.org.na

Municipality
Tel: 290 2911/2693
Fax: 290 2111

Entry Requirements
All visitors must have a valid passport, and temporary residence permits for visitors are issued on arrival and allow tourists a period of 90 days in the country. Bona fide tourists and business travellers from many countries are exempted from visa requirements (enquire with your travel agent). Visitors are, however, advised to confirm visa requirements with their travel agent.

Health Requirements
Vaccinations against smallpox, cholera and yellow fever are not required. However, visitors travelling from or through countries where yellow fever is endemic must have a valid International Certificate of Vaccination. This requirement does not apply to air travellers in transit. No AIDS screening tests are conducted.

Air Travel
Hosea Kutako International Airport, 45km (28 miles) west of the capital, is the major point of entry into Namibia. Eros Airport, 4km (2.5 miles) from the city centre, is served by domestic flights. Air Namibia, the national carrier, has regular scheduled flights to Katima Mulilo, Lüderitz, Ondangwa, Oranjemund, Swakopmund and Walvis Bay. There are landing strips throughout the country and air-charter services are available in Windhoek, Swakopmund and Walvis Bay.

Road Travel
Namibia has a well-developed road system, covering some 40,000km (24,856 miles). Trunk roads covering 5000km (3107 miles) are tarred and connect all the main centres, while major gravel-surface roads are generally in a good condition. The state of district and farm roads varies from good to poor, depending on when they were last graded.

MOTORING TIPS: During the summer months care should be exercised on gravel-surface roads as washaways are common after rains. Motorists should look out for wild or domestic animals as they can cause serious accidents. Warthogs feed in the long grass alongside the road and are in the habit of suddenly crossing it. Kudu are a danger at night in densely vegetated areas, and warning signs should be heeded. In rural areas, domestic animals are not fenced so be careful. Always carry emergency spares and sufficient water (at least 10 litres; 2.6 gallons), especially on the lonely backroads.
Driver's licence: The carrying of driver's licences is now compulsory. Foreign licences are acceptable if they carry a photograph and are either printed in English or accompanied by an English-language certificate of authenticity. An alternative is to obtain an International Driving Permit before departing for Namibia. Licences issued in Botswana, Lesotho, South Africa, Swaziland and Zimbabwe are valid.

ROAD RULES AND SIGNS: In Namibia one drives on the left-hand side of the road. The speed limit on major roads is 120kph (75mph) and in urban areas 60kph (37mph), unless otherwise indicated. Depending on the condition of gravel-surface roads, the recommended speed is between 80kph (50mph)

Resources

and 100kph (62mph). All proclaimed routes are numbered (major routes with the prefix B, secondary routes with prefix C, district roads with prefix D and farm roads with prefix P or F), and tourist attractions are generally well marked.

CAR HIRE: Avis, Budget and Imperial are represented in Windhoek with branches at Hosea Kutako International Airport and at Swakopmund or Walvis Bay. Several companies specialize in four-wheel-drive vehicles, and Britz: Namibia rents out campervans. Insurance: Third-party insurance is included in the price of fuel. The excess for damage to hired vehicles is high as most driving is on gravel roads with high accident rates. When making reservations, establish the excess and the renter's responsibility in respect of collision damage waiver insurance.

PETROL: Petrol is available at filling stations throughout Namibia. In Windhoek and some of the larger towns fuel is available 24 hours a day, but in some of the smaller towns and settlements pumps close at 18:00, while restricted hours could apply during weekends. The availability of fuel at some settlements in remote areas is unreliable at times and you should ensure that you have sufficient fuel to get to your destination. In the northwest of Namibia petrol is available only at Ruacana, Sesfontein and Opuwo. Cash only is accepted for petrol in rural areas.

AUTOMOBILE ASSOCIATION OF NAMIBIA: The AAN office is in the Carl List Building, on the corner of Independence Avenue and Fidel Castro Street, tel: (061) 224201. The AA has tow-in service contractors in all major towns. The after-hours breakdown number is: (061) 224201. Maps of Namibia and other southern African countries are also available.
Coach travel: Intercape Mainliner operates a luxury coach service between Windhoek and Walvis Bay, and between Windhoek and Victoria Falls. There are also regular coach departures from the capital to Cape Town and Johannesburg in South Africa.

What to Wear

During the day dress is usually casual, but in some of the more sophisticated hotel restaurants and bars, jeans, T-shirts and slip-slops are not acceptable in the evening when 'smart casual' clothes are the norm. Early mornings and evenings can be cold during winter (May to September), so pack warm clothing such as trousers, long-sleeved shirts, a jersey or anorak. During the hot summer months (October to April) loose-fitting clothes, a wide-rimmed hat and a raincoat are essential. After rain, temperatures drop by quite a few degrees so include a light jersey for the occasional cool summer evening. Mosquitoes can be troublesome during summer, so remember to pack loose-fitting trousers and long-sleeved shirts to protect legs and arms during the evenings. Warm clothing is necessary throughout the year along the coast where fog and a chilly breeze can create unpleasant conditions.

Medical Services

It is advisable to take out medical insurance before your departure for Namibia. Windhoek has three private hospitals (the Roman Catholic Hospital in Werner List Street, Medi-Clinic in Erospark and the Rhino Park Private Hospital), there is a Medi-Clinic in Otjiwarongo, and Swakopmund has the Cottage Private Hospital. Walvis Bay has the Welwitschia Hospital. Some churches in the north of the country run hospitals or clinics, and there are state hospitals in major towns. Membership of International SOS, a company which specializes in dealing with medical emergencies countrywide, is highly advisable, tel: (061) 231236, fax: 231254.

DOCTORS: Private doctors in Windhoek are listed under 'Medical practitioners' in the telephone directory.

PHARMACIES: All major towns have pharmacies, usually open during normal business hours; some pharmacies in Windhoek have extended trading hours. In rural areas medication is often available only from the state hospital or clinic.

Security

As a rule it is quite safe to walk around the streets of Windhoek and other towns after dark without fear of being attacked, although isolated incidents do occur from time to time so some basic precautions are advisable. Avoid looking like the typical tourist, do not carry large amounts of cash on your person and hand valuables in for safekeeping at hotels. In some rural areas petty thieving has become a problem, so do not leave camping gear and other valuables unattended; rather lock them away.

Information courtesy of
the Globetrotter Guide to Namibia
by Willie Olivier,
published by New Holland Publishers.